Patterns of Equality

The Influence of New Structures in European Higher Education upon the Equality of Educational Opportunity

Guy Neave

NFER Publishing Company Ltd

Published by the NFER Publishing Company Ltd.,
2 Jennings Buildings, Thames Avenue,
Windsor, Berks. SL4 1QS
Registered Office: The Mere, Upton Park, Slough SL1 2DQ
First published 1976
© European Cultural Foundation, 1976
ISBN 0 85633 114 7

Printed in Great Britain by
Whitefriars Press, Medway Wharf Road, Tonbridge, Kent TN9 1QR

Distributed in the USA by Humanities Press Inc.,
Atlantic Highlands, New Jersey 07716 USA.

Contents

This book was originally a report to the European Commission prepared by the Institute of Education of the European Cultural Foundation. The Institute prepares reports on behalf of the Commission and other bodies, all of which are published. More details of these publications and of the Institute's journal *Paedagogica Europea* may be had from:

The Publications Officer,
Institute of Education,
Foundation Européenne de la Culture,
Université Dauphine,
Place du Maréchal de Lattre de Tassigny,
75116 Paris.

PREFACE

Anyone who brings up the issue of equality of educational opportunity must be aware of the strong emotions it arouses, the interests which, seemingly, it attacks and the implications that it holds for the future shape of society. This is as true for higher education as for secondary reorganization which I have written about elsewhere.

Alongside this eternal controversy in education, current debate has turned in another direction. The various aspects of manpower planning are, what with the present economic crisis, moving once again to the forefront of the educational stage. During the research prior to the writing of this report on the new structures in European higher education, it became increasingly evident to me that the fundamental issue at stake revolved around the apparently irreconcilable conflict between these two aspects of educational development. Since this whole area is of growing — and vital — interest to the United Kingdom, I have added a postscript to the original document. There were two purposes in doing this: first, to provide a conclusion of special relevance to the British context; and second, though more as a hope, to provide a European perspective to the debate which has often tended to rely more on the myths of European education systems than on what really is taking place in them.

I should add, however, that the views expressed are none but my own. The study was supported by the European Commission. That they have been pleased to permit its publication in no way suggests their acceptance of what I have said. Copies of the main corpus of the report will be made available by the Commission in the other languages of the European Community.

I should in particular like to thank Dr Ladislav Cerych, Director of the European Cultural Foundation's *Institut d'Education*, who has created a unique intellectual environment which makes this sort of study possible; Ms Annie Maniquet who typed the manuscript and Dr Sally Jenkinson, Senior Lecturer in Politics at the Polytechnic of North London, who helped me to write the British postscript.

This is an appropriate opportunity to thank also those people whose previous work or whose advice contributed significantly to the preparation of this book. Amongst them are the following:

M Michel BERNARD Département Gestion de l'Enterprise,
         IUT Nantes, France
Mrs Caroline COX   Department of Sociology,
         Polytechnic of North London, England

Mme Dorothea FURTH	OECD, Rue André Pascal, Paris, France
Professor Gunther HARTFIEL	Department of Sociology and Education, Gesamthochschule Kassel, West Germany
Dr Olav MAGNUSSEN	Department of Economics, Rogaland Distrikt Hogskole, Stavanger, Norway
Mr Maurice MEALING	Department of Sociology, Polytechnic of North London, England
Mrs Naomi McINTOSH	Pro Vice-Chancellor, The Open University, Milton Keynes, England
Frau NAÜSEL	Central Administration, Gesamthochschule Kassel, West Germany
M. J.-P. PELLEGRIN	OECD, Rue André Pascal, Paris, France
Professor Maurice PESTON	Department of Economics, Queen Mary College, London, England

Guy Neave
Paris, July 1976

Part One

The Evolution of Higher Education
1945 – 1975

Chapter 1

General Developments in Higher Education in the Post-War Period

Introduction

The purpose of this report is to analyse and to assess the influence that certain new structures in higher education have had upon the equality of educational opportunity. The creation of new structures in higher education represents what one might term the second stage in its post-war development which, to a large extent, was dictated by problems engendered in the first. Hence, it is important to identify firstly the common characteristics of the first stage and the problems it threw up; and, in the second place, to see in what way the second stage in fact was able to meet, palliate or resolve them.

Broadly speaking, the first stage in the development of higher education post 1945, involved its quantitative expansion within a traditional framework. In other words, the modes of access, qualifications, and types of study remained in a mould that, historically, has been associated with the role of the university as an instrument for the formation of an elite through theoretical studies, carried out on a full time basis. During this first phase which may be seen as roughly coterminous with the period 1959 to 1967 – though naturally the period may alter depending on the circumstances in a particular country – reform involved no major qualitative change. What it did involve, rather, was more students overcoming the historic barriers that regulated entry to higher education. The barriers themselves remained in place. In short, higher education was not so much a vehicle or an active instrument for educational reform as the recipient of changes that took place lower down the educational system in the secondary school. Previous studies undertaken by the OECD have suggested that three main factors were at work in secondary schools to bring about expansion in higher education. First, the development of systems of secondary education in which selection for the 'academic' track leading to higher education was delayed. Such was the case in France, Norway and Sweden, for instance. The second combination of factors involved an increase in the number of students in a particular age group who entered those streams preparing for university entry. Such was the trend observable in Germany and the Netherlands. The third pattern of development involved an increase in the number of school leavers qualified to enter university and, simultaneously, a reduction in the number of early leavers and drop outs. Into such a pattern fell Austria, Denmark, England and Wales. (1)

Characteristics of the first phase in the post-war development of higher education

In consequence, the first phase of development in higher education had, as its main impetus, reform in secondary education which in turn generated or stimulated a greater social demand to which higher education responded by providing more places. Government policy tended to limit itself to responding to this situation by providing new places in higher education, without seeking to alter either its structure or the traditional relationship between the university at the apex of the educational pyramid or its relationship with other patterns of institution. Indeed, the one feature that underlay the first stage of development was what one might term the 'policy of the institutional constant'.

The 'policy of the institutional constant' is an important concept and merits additional explanation since it lay at the heart of both curriculum development — or lack of it during this time — and also a certain notion of educational opportunity. This concept formed, effectively, the main instrument by which the university assured its historic role of educating an elite, by dint of the voluntary self elimination of students at various points in their course. Since this elimination was assumed to be on grounds of ability or intellectual weakness, the basic theory that linked the student to his course of study was one which the latter was the constant and the former the variable. Hence, the definition of an elite was determined by the extent to which the student could adapt himself to a 'traditional' curriculum, rather than the converse. Thus the continuation of 'traditional' modes of teaching, content of courses and organization of study could be justified on the grounds that without it, the university could not assure its function of the production of a meritocracy. Similarly, the policy of the 'institutional constant' played an important role in defining certain notions about the equality of educational opportunity.

As conceived during the first phase of post-war development in higher education, equality of educational opportunity rested on a *logistical* interpretation. Or, put in more routine terms, it rested on the notion that every school leaver so qualified should be able to continue in higher education, an interpretation which reached its best expression in the recommendations of the Robbins Report in the UK (1963). It was a logistical interpretation for the simple reason that its realization depended simply on the greater provision of places. It did not, for instance, conceive of higher education playing a compensatory role for certain social groups which, for various reasons, missed out in the final stages of secondary education. The logistical definition of equality of educational opportunity took for granted that higher education should build upon the inequalities of secondary education. Hence, the equality of educational opportunity, influenced by the notion of the 'institutional constant' consisted merely in providing the same educational experience to more school leavers who desired it.

Characteristics of the second phase in post-war development of higher education

The motives behind the introduction of the second phase in the development of higher education are highly complex. We will examine them in greater detail in the course of this report. Suffice it to say that the main motives were, *grosso modo*, three. First, considerations of an economic nature, and concern about the implications of educational development on the future manpower needs of countries; second, a more egalitarian interpretation of the equality of educational opportunity; third, and a consequence of the first two, the realization that reform in higher education required pedagogic and institutional innovation as well. Thus, the second phase involved both qualitative change as well as structural innovation. Characteristic of this stage in the development of higher education was the tendency for higher education to become firstly, the active agent of educational reform, rather than remaining parasitic upon change lower down the education system; secondly, it involved a higher degree of government intervention, through the setting up of new institutional patterns, regulating the new relationship between traditional and 'new structures' and, in some cases, though by no means all, determining the educational task and the objectives of the new bodies.

This phase, which began in France in 1966 with the creation of the first Instituts Universitaires de Technologie, in the UK with the White Paper *A Plan for Polytechnics and other Colleges* of the same year may be seen as a break with the previous pattern of government policy. In seeking better ways to diversify higher education and to improve the articulation of post-secondary education, government action no longer endorsed a policy of the institutional constant. Effectively, the main thrust of the second stage which still remains uncompleted, was to push post-secondary education from being institution-based to becoming network-based, or, alternatively, from a pattern grounded on the concept of institutional autonomy to one in which post-secondary and higher education functions as an interlocking system (2). Whilst there are reasons for viewing this change in policy as a break from the predominant stance taken by governments during the previous phase, there are, nevertheless, other reasons for considering it as part of an ongoing process and as a continuation of a deeply laid feature of contemporary education.

Seen from the standpoint of continuity, rather than change, both phases of expansion and diversification represent an increasing centrality of education in determining the future economic and social structure in a particular country. Active government intervention in determining economic and social objectives for new types of institution is, then, simply the recognition of a long historical process by which control over the means of production is gained by control over the means of education. Yet beneath this apparent continuity, the creation of 'new structures' of higher education, whether in the non-university sector or, as in the case of the German *Gesamthochschule* or the British Open University, in the university sector represents a fundamental change in the role of higher education. The establishment of a variety of methods of access to higher education, through different 'routes', the diversity of study modes — full-time, part-time, sandwich courses, corresponds firstly to a break in the temporal structure of higher education. It is, in short, no longer dependent on following on sequentially from secondary education. It also entails, in some instances, a divorce of teaching from the physical structure as well, as in the case of the Open University. From the standpoint of both curriculum and pedagogy, the priorities and relationships that governed previous university structures have been reversed. In short, the burden of the second phase from a curriculum as well as from a pedagogic standpoint is to render the student as the constant and to alter the curriculum according to his or her particular needs. As such, it should then, be regarded as the penetration into higher education of that process of individualization of the curriculum that is at present underway in secondary education.

The manner in which this general tendency is realized alters from country to country. In some cases, it involves an integration of hitherto separate domains of higher education to permit students easy transfer from one sector to another. This pattern we might term the 'comprehensive solution'. Essentially it involves administrative change rather than change in the content of courses, though, of course, it does not exclude this possibility. Another method, of individualizing the options open to students is through partial integration of different sectors through courses that lead from short cycle to long cycle university institutes. Such was the pattern adopted in Yugoslavia in the early Sixties with regard to the *Vise Skole* and is at present under way in Norway in the form of the district college. Otherwise known as the 'multi-purpose' model, it permits the assimilation of courses in one institute into the first two years of university study, as well as providing general and vocational education within the framework of the two year college (3). Essentially, these two models involve the setting up of a network of courses by permitting student transfer from one to another. A third pattern, which one finds in Britain, involves the creation of diversity inside one particular institution, separate from the university, and providing both academic and vocational education within the confines of a single institution, namely the polytechnics.

The legislative aspect

The degree to which these patterns present a specific response to a new definition of educational opportunity depends, to a large degree on the aims, objectives and purposes laid upon them by legislation. The legislative aspect is highly significant. Firstly, because it defines the official purpose of the particular institution in a manner far more explicit than the various instruments of government which created the traditional university. For that reason, the task of the new structures is far more explicit than the vague and general roles of scholarship and inquiry that have been attributed to their predecessors. Secondly, legislation allows us to ascertain the particular criteria on which the structures it sets up, may be judged, their success noted and their failures identified.

The relevance of the legislative side goes far beyond a mere statement of official intent. For whilst it can tell us about the main considerations prompting the reform, it can also provide us with insight into the relationship between governments and their creations as well as the manner in which reform is introduced. In addition, it may also tell us much about the way a particular education system functions. This too is important. For if the identification of common trends, tendencies and characteristics is implicit in studies of an international nature, it is equally relevant to consider how similar results may be attained by the use of vastly different means.

Since the main burden of this report is to examine the extent to which new structures in higher education have contributed to the equalization of educational opportunity, the implicit assumption is that legislation *can* bring specific sociological change. This is not quite the same order of priority as existed, for instance, during the former phase of development in higher education. Then, legislation, as we have pointed out, had simply the onus of *responding* to, or retrospectively recognizing, sociological change that was already in train. Here, on the contrary, legislation involves an implied theory of educational, social or economic development that is desirable but which has not yet taken place. Effectively, legislation relating to new structures in higher education is *prospective*, in an attempt to bring about a new situation. Hence, the role of educational legislation also underwent change during the second phase of post-war development of higher education.

The role of 'covert forces' in the development of 'new structures'

But legislation is not the only way by which the tasks and objectives of educational institutions are formulated, though obviously it is — theoretically — the easiest way so to do. Institutions are dynamic, undergo change, often in response to developments which initial legislation did not foresee, just as there are forces — economic in the main — that could conceivably contribute to the success of particular types of institution, as a function of 'spin off'. Indeed, in a period when a premium is placed upon innovation in all sectors of secondary and post-secondary education, the influence that non-legislative factors might play in altering the role of newly established institutions could well be greater than before. Hence, we need to see to what extent the evolution of the 'new structures' over a period of time has, if at all, involved any deviation from their more official objectives, what precisely those forces were, and what, if any, were their consequences. Perhaps, the most powerful of these is the interpretation of the official role entrusted to them by their personnel. How far does this accord with the original intentions of governments? What changes have had subsequently to be brought about in the 'new structures' and for what reasons? In fine, what evidence is there of adaptation amongst the new structures of higher education after the legislative parameters have been defined? This is a crucial question, not simply because it may afford insights into the manner in which educational opportunity is — or is not being realized, but because the creation of these institutions in the first place sprang from the belief that the university in its traditional form, was not capable of meeting the new demands society placed upon it.

The way in which flexibility was conceived with regard to these establishments will be dealt with later in the course of the report. But, however envisaged, flexibility whether defined *vis à vis* the opportunities open to the individual student or whether defined in terms of the institutional response to external social and economic change, must logically, be a two edged sword. The ability of an institution to meet broad social change does not necessarily mean that it will meet, interpret or respond to 'the right' change. Or that the way it meets such change is necessarily in keeping with the government's official policy. But flexibility can just as well mean the capacity to react to the 'wrong' change as well. For what is deemed to be a positive response can just as well be a deviation when viewed from the standpoint of a different social or political perspective. What is one man's process of democratization is another's expenditure of public funds! Flexibility, more than ever, raises the question of the particular series of values or ideologies by which an institution is governed.

The structure of the report

This report is divided into three main parts. The first deals with the general evolution of higher education over the past thirty years from two perspectives. There are the qualitative trends in enrolment and the various proposals which have been put forward for structural innovation by member governments of the EEC. The second part deals with the growth of new structures in higher education and comprises the major bulk of the empirical analysis undertaken for this inquiry. More specifically, the second part — itself subdivided into four chapters — begins by examining some of the purposes which have been officially ascribed to our target institutions. These institutions are:

1. the Instituts Universitaires de Technologie;
2. the Gesamthochschule Kassel;
3. the Norwegian District Colleges;
4. the Open University in the United Kingdom;
5. the Polytechnics in England and Wales;
6. the Vise Skole in Yugoslavia.

However, before we can undertake a detailed examination of the extent to which these so called 'New Structures' have — or alternatively, have not — contributed towards the equalizing of educational opportunity we need to look a little more closely at this concept itself. What do we mean by equality of educational opportunity? Does this term in fact describe one particular set of criterion variables by which one may judge the degree to which an education system is moving towards such a goal? Or are there, on the contrary, different and perhaps contradictory interpretations of this same phenomenon hidden beneath the wrappings of this otherwise anodine expression? Chapter Five offers a clarification of this issue and also sets out some criterion variables that might be involved in assessing institutional achievement in this area.

Chapter 6 of the Second Part examines the 'new structures' in terms of the conditions of access each demands of its potential entrants. This is an important aspect since it allows us, at least formally, to gauge how far each type of institution possesses a latitude or, alternatively, a discretion to operate various strategies that might admit groups of students who, for one reason or for another might otherwise have been excluded from access to higher education. Chapter 7 represents the main thrust of the analysis in which the composition of the student body in each of our component institutions is examined and compared to its counterpart in the 'classical' university of each respective country. The two main criterion variables used in the assessment are: first, the educational background of students and, second, their social class background.

The Third Part of the Report consists of a summary in which some of the salient points that have arisen in the body of the report are brought together to shed light on the general problems that arise if and when one wishes to formulate policy in a similar domain. This, the final part, is presented as a synthesis of some of the major problems faced by the 'new structures'. It may also be seen from another angle — namely as an elucidation of some of the difficulties that one is likely to meet if the decision is taken to implement in the field of higher education, strategies for equalizing opportunity. In addition the report contains suggestions with respect of future research in this general area as well as a list of certain statistical indicators to aid such an enterprise.

Chapter 2

The Quantitative Expansion of Higher Education 1965 - 1974

Introduction

In the previous chapter we looked at the general issues posed by the second phase of post-war development in higher education. In this chapter we turn our attention to the quantitative dimensions of change. Accordingly, our task is to place the evolution of 'new structures' against the broader, but nonetheless important context of student flows into post-secondary education. We have termed the first phase in post war development the 'phase of expansion'. Whilst the second witnessed the elaboration of new priorities in the policies of governments *vis à vis* higher education, expansion did not, for all that, cease. Consequently, we need to know to what degree growth in the various component sectors — university or non-university — continued, accelerated or declined. By the same token we need to know to what extent quantitative expansion differed, or altered amongst the university and the non-university domains between the period 1965 to 1974.

Methodology

There are a number of indicators at our disposal which allow an assessment of trends over time. The first and most obvious of these is absolute numbers in higher education. The second is the proportion entering higher education of a given age cohort. The third involves what is commonly termed the transfer ratio. This is usually expressed in percentage form and represents the proportion of those who obtained the requisite school leaving qualifications entering university. A fourth indicator, to some extent already anticipated by the concept of 'transfer ratios' is the proportion of school leavers in a particular age group attaining the school leaving certificate. And finally, though by no means of lesser significance, are alterations in the ratio of men to women in higher education, this latter often acting as a crude indicator of the degree to which education systems tend towards equality of educational opportunity in such a domain.

Before we embark upon a detailed analysis based on these criteria one should bear in mind that realistic growth indices should be calculated on the basis of *level* of study, not on *institutional* type. To explain the difference, take the case of the United Kingdom. One may enrol for degree level courses in various types of institutions — universities, polytechnics and colleges of education. To compare growth rates initially at least, on an institutional basis assumes that such institutions are compatible. In many cases this is not so. In some cases their level of study is fully equivalent to that found at university. In others it is not. Compatibility is therefore based upon a concept of 'university level study'. This has been defined by the OECD inquiries as 'a long course (3 or 4 years study at least) entry to which requires full school leaving certificate and which is completed by a first degree leading on to higher degrees'. By contrast, non-university level is regarded as being of relatively short duration, for which entry is not necessarily dependent on a secondary school leaving certificate. Such studies are completed by the award of a diploma at a lower level than the university first degree (4).

Development of higher education from a statistical viewpoint

When examining the expansion and growth of higher education from the 1960s onwards, one should remember the particular circumstance that led towards rapid growth. The coincidence of four major elements — some of which are present today, others not — accounted to a very large extent for the structural transformation that took place over the past decade and a half. These four elements may be summarized as:

1. the arrival of the post-war 'bulge' — exceptionally large age cohorts — at the doors of higher education;
2. the growing need of additional highly trained manpower created by economic expansion as well as the need to sustain high rates of growth through investment in post-secondary education;
3. the particular need of education systems outwith higher education for additional personnel to cope with changes of a structural and a political nature associated with the development of a generalized system of secondary education*

---

*   By 'general system of secondary education' we mean one in which access to post-secondary education is not decided at the passage from primary to secondary education. Hence, it is a system based on non-differentiation between different types of school and thus rejects a bipartite or tripartite model.

4. the demand that access to higher education be opened up to those groups in society that, hitherto had remained relatively excluded.

The coincidence of these elements created an overall policy which, though naturally varying in particular countries, nevertheless endorsed what one may term a policy of growth constant. This important assumption underlay both the first period in the development of post-war higher education in Europe — a period which we have identified with the policy of the institutional constant and its successor, the period of diversification. Recent developments, particularly in the matter of enrolment have suggested that this catechism of 'growth eternal' no longer enjoys the weight of orthodoxy in the educational world.

If one looks at the annual rate of expansion in the numbers enrolled in all sectors of higher education, one sees that the period from around 1970 onward involves a considerable slow down for most countries.* The annual rate of growth is less than half what it had been in 1960 to 1965. The two exceptions to this are Western Germany and Yugoslavia. (See Table 2.1.)

The decline in the rate of expansion is not however, uniform chronologically speaking. A careful perusal of the figures in Table 2.1 shows two distinct groups of countries; the first, those whose decline began relatively early towards the end of the 1960s. Amongst this former group are France, Denmark and the United Kingdom. The second group of countries tended to see the down turn take place slightly later around 1971 instead of between 1968 and 1969. In the latter group are Italy and the Netherlands. We will examine some of the possible contributing causes later in this chapter. Suffice it here to remark that the pattern of development shown in Germany and Yugoslavia appears rather in the nature of a 'lagged response'. In both countries the rate of expansion during the later 60s was amongst the lowest in the West.

Yet the fact that some countries tended to slow down their rate of growth in higher education and others to continue or to enter a phase that others had left raises rather more questions than it answers. Is there, for instance, any difference in growth between the university and the non-university domains hidden beneath the general picture just

---

* The information on which much of the statistics presented in this chapter are based comes from a study currently in train in the Institut d'Education and undertaken by Ignace Hecquet and Christine Verniers: *L'Evolution des flux d'étudiants dans l'enseignement supérieur ... étude entreprise pour l'International Council for Educational Development New York*, Bruxelles, 1975. All tables, unless the source indicates to the contrary, are derived from this document.

Table 2.1: Annual growth rate of enrolments in all sectors of higher education by year and country

Country	N =	1965/66	1966/67	1967/68	1968/69	1969/70	1970/71	1971/72	1972/73	1973/74	1974/75
Belgium	84.000		9.0	9.2	12.3	6.3	–	–	–	6.4	
Denmark	53.225		8.8	8.8	10.6	5.0	5.4	7.5	11.9	4.1	5.3
France	524.878		8.4	12.7	14.7	5.5	3.8	6.9	5.6	1.7	2.0
Germany	384.400		5.8	2.9	6.0	6.8	7.9	17.1	10.6	10.8	7.6
Italy	424.717		12.3	9.4	10.1	11.7	10.7	11.2	5.7	4.6	
Netherlands	152.634		7.4	9.5	8.6	8.5	8.5	7.3	–	–	
UK	432.548		11.1	10.3	6.4	2.8	3.3	2.6	1.5	1.6	
Yugoslavia	184.923		5.7	7.8	9.8	3.6	8.9	8.2	6.8	8.9	9.5

Source: I. Hecquet and C. Verniers, *Evolution des flux d'étudiants dans l'enseignement supérieur . . . étude entreprise pour l'ICDE*, New York, Bruxelles, December 1975.

Table 2.2: Annual growth rate of university and non-university sectors of higher education by year and country (total enrolments)

Country	Base N =	1965/66	1966/67	1967/68	1968/69	1969/70	1970/71	1971/72	1972/73	1973/74	1974/75
Belgium											
u/v	48.800		10.2	10.0	9.5	7.5	7.9	7.9	3.9	2.1	1.9
non u/v	35.200		7.3	8.0	16.3	4.7	–	–	–	12.7	–
Denmark											
u/v	28.859		11.4	12.5	5.5	7.4	8.7	9.1	8.9	5.0	4.9
non u/v	23.366		5.5	3.8	18.0	2.0	0.8	5.0	16.6	2.7	5.9
France											
u/v	433.960		10.0	13.5	15.6	4.6	3.8	6.5	5.1	0.8	2.1
non u/v	90.918		1.0	8.6	10.3	10.4	3.8	8.9	8.2	6.0	1.6
Germany											
u/v	299.700		7.0	3.2	6.6	6.5	9.1	13.7	15.1	10.6	5.5
non u/v	84.700		1.4	1.7	3.8	7.2	3.3	31.1	-5.2	11.8	16.2
Italy											
u/v	412.366		12.1	9.7	10.4	12.0	10.8	11.3	5.8	4.5	
non u/v	12.351		18.2	0.7	2.4	-0.1	3.5	3.8	2.1	8.9	
Netherlands											
u/v	64.409		10.6	9.3	8.8	10.4	10.4	9.2	–	–	–
non u/v	88.225		5.0	9.7	8.5	7.0	6.9	5.7	3.3	4.2	4.3
U.K.											
u/v	208.800		14.1	9.8	8.0	5.9	4.3	4.2	2.9	2.6	–
non u/v	223.748		8.3	10.7	4.9	-0.3	2.2	0.9	-0.1	0.4	–
Yugoslavia											
u/v	116.273		3.3	6.8	15.0	9.7	11.3	7.7	8.3	11.6	7.2
non u/v	68.650		9.7	9.6	1.7	-7.2	4.0	9.2	3.4	2.6	15.1

Source: Hecquet et Verniers, *op. cit., tableaux de synthèse.*

described? Has the non-university sector developed more rapidly in recent years or is the slow down a general phenomenon throughout higher education? Over the five year period from 1965 to 1970, expansion was greatest in the university sector. This tendency appears to have been reversed during the early 1970s. In certain countries, Belgium, France and the Netherlands, growth in higher education hides what one might term a steady state situation relatively speaking in the university sector. By contrast, expansion has been due to growth in the non-university areas. (Hecquet and Verniers, *op. cit.*, p. 14.)

As we shall see later this tendency is also present in the UK where the universities in the normally accepted sense of the word have been in a situation of nil growth. Degree level study has, however, seen considerable expansion in the polytechnics though to what extent this is due to a change in direction of student flows from university is difficult to say. Recent studies conducted within the Scottish context, in which the strength of the non-university sector is much less pronounced than in England, for example, suggests there is some reason for thinking that diversion from university into non-university institutions for degree level study has, in fact, taken place (6),

But this is a very particular phenomenon. It is more developed in the ease of working class students — girls especially — and those of relatively low measured performance in the School Leaving Certificate. This suggests that such changes in direction are more in the nature of a conjunctural effect, the result of fears of graduate unemployment pushing applicants towards 'relevant' courses. How far it will be sustained is a different matter. Nor is it possible to state at this juncture, to what extent similar considerations lie beneath parallel trends in other countries. Most certainly, the Scottish example points to a considerable transformation in the types of institution to which school leavers *apply*. Generally, this involves a marked move away from applications limited to the university sector and a rise in what one might call cross-institutional applications (7). These patterns are not without interest. They allow us, though within a context limited to the UK, to dismiss the thesis according to which change in student flows follows from structural reorganization in higher education. The non-university sector in Scotland, and the Central Institutions (polytechnics' equivalents) especially, has undergone far less development than its English and Welsh counterparts. Nevertheless, in all three countries, England, Wales and Scotland, the flow into the non-university sector degree level study has grown. In fine, the crucial common element would appear to be less the power of attraction of the reorganized sector so much as the lack of attraction of the university. Again, how far this is so in a broader European context is difficult to assess.

If it should be an important consideration, then it is certainly less marked in the case of Germany and Denmark where the evolution of the university and non-university sector has continued at approximately the same rate for both domains. By contrast, Yugoslavia shows the university continuing to expand its enrolment far faster than the non-university sector.

Age groups entering higher education

The use of the proportion of an age group entering higher education though useful in a general sense, does not, of course, explain the reasons why, for instance, one country should have a higher proportion than another. Nor does it serve particularly well in enabling one to judge the effectiveness of various policy actions. It does, on the other hand, allow one to observe the rate of development over similar time spans either within a particular country or between different countries. Table 2.3 sets out the number of qualified school leavers entering higher education as a proportion of particular age groups for the countries under investigation.

Table 2.3: Qualified entrants to higher education as percentage of the relevant age group

Country	Age Group	1965	1970	1972	1973	1974
Belgium	18—20	21.8	29.5	—	—	—
Denmark	19—21	16.8	24.1	—	—	—
France[1]	18—20	14.8	19.2	24.6	25.9	—
Germany	20—22	11.6	15.3	19.5	—	—
Italy	19—21	14.8[2]	27.9	—	—	29.2
Netherlands	17—20	12.8	18.3	—	—	—
UK	18—19	12.4	20.3	21.3	21.4	—

Sources: I. Hecquet et C. Verniers, *op. cit.*; J.P. Pellegrin 'Quantitative trends in post secondary education 1960—1970', *Towards Mass Higher Education, issues and dilemmas*, Paris, 1974, OCDE, p. 37.

The picture that emerges is somewhat disparate and varies widely depending on the country one cares to examine. Nevertheless, it is probably true to say that, taken over all, higher education systems within the EEC have, by 1973, passed the point at which, quantitatively speaking they remain elite forming. If, for instance, one assumes that in 1965 all higher education systems were still within their traditional mould, accepting only an extremely small minority of the age group, it is evident that there has been a considerable improvement in the chances of students in such a group gaining access to higher education. Of course, it may be argued that this is as much due to demographic factors — notably the decline in the birth rate subsequent to the passage of the post-war 'bulge' through the education system — as it is to sheer expansion in the number of places available. Even so, despite the tendency for the proportion of the age group entering higher education to level out in recent years, it remains a fact that the chances of such an age cohort continuing its education have improved by between 50 per cent and, in the case of Italy, by almost 100 per cent over the ten year period from 1965.

Strictly speaking the use of measurements such as numbers entering higher education expressed as a percentage of the relevant age group is not an educational indicator. Rather it is a demographic measurement, which assumes the education system to be a sub-system within a series of complex flows between the world of the school room and the world of work, training, personal development and leisure. Or seen from another standpoint it may be regarded as an actuarial indicator for calculating an individual's 'life chances'. Hence, the influence of component sub-systems within the general social system can be assessed in the light of performance and achievement in other areas, for instance, the economic domain. In this case such a measurement merely acts as a means of estimating the effect upon the individual of a sub-system in society through which he has passed previously upon his fortunes in another area of society in which he is at present. What we require, by contrast, is a more precise *educational* indicator to illustrate the trends underlying the passage of aggregates from one part of the education system — for example the secondary sector — to another for example, higher education. For only if we examine *educational* indicators can we resolve the apparent paradox contained in the slow down in the growth rates of higher education and the increase in the proportion of the age cohort gaining access to it.

Such indicators can be said to be:

  i. the number of school leavers qualified for entry to higher education as a percentage of the age cohort;
 ii. the transfer rate of these students to higher education.

Trends and flows to higher education amongst qualified school leavers
In Table 2.4 the number of qualified school leavers is presented as a percentage of the relevant age group.

Regardless of the particular policies endorsed by the various countries in the secondary sector, the general picture is towards a higher proportion of the age group reaching the standard necessary for access to higher education. From 1970 onwards, however, the growth rate in qualified school leavers has slowed up, all over Europe with the exceptions of Germany where the rhythm continues — and the

Table 2.4: Qualified school leavers as a portion of the relevant age group by year and by country

Country	1964 / 65	1969 / 70	1971 / 72	1972 / 73	1973 / 74
			percentage of age group		
Belgium 1*	—	17.1	—	20.1	19.6
2	30.1	—	—	34.2	35.0
Denmark 1	10.3	16.3	—	21.2	—
France 1	12.6	16.3	17.8	18.3	18.6
2	—	20.6	23.0	23.7	—
Germany 1*	8.9	12.3	—	14.0	—
2**	—	11.0	—	17.4	19.0
Italy 1	—	27.3	32.6	32.6	33.0
Netherlands 1	9.7	16.6	21.4	19.4	—
UK 1	10.7	13.6	14.4	—	—
2	18.8	23.1	24.8	—	—

Source: Hecquet et Verniers, *op. cit.*, Table 4, pp. 30—1.

Netherlands where the proportion of qualified students fell from 21.4 per cent of the age group to 19.4 per cent during the school years 1971 / 2 and 1972 / 3.

However, that more school leavers attain the requisite qualifications to enter higher education does not mean that of necessity they continue their studies. As a final piece in the jigsaw, we need to know what, if any, change has taken place in the proportion of qualified students continuing and actually entering higher education. In this context, we examine the second indicator, namely the transfer rate of qualified school leavers for higher education. This is set out in Table 2.5.

Table 2.5: Transfer ratio of qualified students entering higher education as percentage of those qualified the previous year (by year and country)

Country	1965	1970	1973	1974
Belgium	64.1	70.5	61.2	63.4
Denmark	78.9	80.3	76.7	
France (univ. only)			81.1	79.2
Germany (univ. only)	92.9	81.2	84.9	
Italy	78.3	84.6	85.5	88.4
Netherlands	55.5	50.0		35.3
UK (universities only)	64.8	63.1	60.9	

Source: Hecquet et Verniers, *op. cit.*, Table 5.
University level study only*

If we divide the period 1965 to 1974 into two — before and after 1970 — and group various countries according to whether their transfer ratio increased, remained stable or decreased during these periods, we find overall that during the first period 1965–70, the tendency has been for the transfer ratio to increase for three countries — Belgium, Denmark and Italy. In the case of the UK it remained stable, and decreased in Germany and the Netherlands. During the second period, post 1970 it increased in Germany and Italy, remained stable in Belgium, France and the United Kingdom, declined in Denmark and the Netherlands. Interestingly, in the case of the UK where one can separate out the transfer ratio to universities *stricto sensu*, we find a marked decline in the proportion of qualified school leavers entering that sector, even though, from an overall perspective the proportion entering university *level* courses of study remains comparatively stable. This development is not all that surprising in view of what we suggested was taking place in the Scottish education system during this period, namely a diversion of students who previously would have entered university, into other institutes of higher education. It is also perfectly in keeping with government policy to diversify higher education and to switch students away from the university sector.

Changes in the ratio of boys to girls in the student body

It is generally held that one of the groups which is discriminated against in access to higher education are women. And hence, many studies involving the equality of education opportunity and its evolution pay careful attention to the ratio of men to women in the various sectors of higher education. Recent work in the Scottish context has, however, revealed another dilemma associated with the more simplistic view of equating educational opportunity with the male / female ratio. That more women enter higher education is not necessarily a sign of more equality if those women happen to come from the more privileged classes of society. For if women constitute a group which is discriminated against, so working class women, by the same token, form a group that is doubly discriminated against, as much by their sex as by their social class background. In Scotland, though there is no reason to suspect that such a phenomenon might not be as developed elsewhere, the drive of women into the university sector during the ten years from 1962 to 1972 has had, as one of the more unforeseen consequences, the driving out of working class men (8). Yet no one can deny, least of all those concerned to realize a greater measure of educational opportunity in higher education, that working class students are not heavily underrepresented, in higher education. This is, of course, no reason why women should continue to be under-represented in higher education either. But one should perhaps, be somewhat wary of believing that improvement in one particular aspect of educational opportunity involves an overall improvement as if the other dimensions remained constant.

Having said this, we turn our attention to the development of higher education with respect to changes in the sex composition of its student body. Table 2.6 sets out the proportion of women in the student body for various countries and for various levels of study, university and non-university level over the decade 1965 to 1974.

From this it may be seen that, generally speaking, women constituted between 25 and 30 per cent of all enrolled students in higher education at the beginning of the period, around 1965 / 6. By the mid 1970s their position improved to between 30 and 40 per cent of all higher education students. This general picture conceals some interesting differences between countries and between the two sectors of higher education — university and non-university. The most marked amelioration is to be seen in Germany which, in 1965 had the lowest proportion of women in higher education of all the countries under investigation — 24 per cent. *Grosso modo*, with the exception of Italy, the non-university sector seems to have borne the brunt of 'feminization', the ratio of women to men improving more rapidly than in the university sector. Such a pattern is to be seen in Germany, Denmark, the Netherlands and the United Kingdom. Given that a major element in non-university level study consists of teacher training — a field which, by tradition has a heavy weighting of women — it is perhaps not unexpected that the phenomenon should be the most developed in this sector, rather than the university level courses. On the other hand, despite the increased female participation in higher education, the relative differences in the proportion of men to women between the university and non-university sectors seem to have grown larger in Italy, Denmark, the Netherlands and the United Kingdom. Take the case of Denmark as illustration of this process. In 1965 / 6 the non-university sector had just under nine per cent more women in its total student body than the university levels of study. By 1973 / 4, this had grown to 18.6 per cent. A similar development may be detected in the United Kingdom, where the 'female participation rate' between the two levels of study widened from around nine per cent in 1966 / 7 to 12 per cent in 1973 / 4. In other words, despite the larger proportion of women in higher education, the relative differentiation between the two sectors does not seem to have decreased.

Nevertheless, despite the continuation of this apparent stratification by sex in higher education, the increase in the number of women students over the past decade has been extremely important. For, as a recent report pointed out, the continued high growth rate amongst women entrants was instrumental in keeping up the overall growth rate

Table 2.6: Proportion of female students in higher education by level of study year and country (all enrolments)

Country		1965/66	1966/67	1967/68	1968/69	1969/70	1970/71	1971/72	1972/73	1973/74	1974/75
Belgium	univ. level	23.9	24.8	26.1	26.9	27.7	28.6	29.5	30.4	31.6	32.6
	non-univ.	45.0	44.9	45.1	45.7	46.2	—	—	50.6	51.2	—
	overall	32.8	33.1	33.8	34.8	35.4	—	—	38.5	39.9	—
Denmark	univ. level	30.3	30.2	31.2	30.9	30.9	31.9	32.8	33.8	33.3	—
	non-univ.	38.9	39.5	40.4	45.0	44.8	43.1	44.2	46.8	51.9	—
	overall	34.0	34.2	34.9	41.2	36.8	36.5	37.3	39.1	40.8	—
France	univ. level	41.4	42.0	42.6	35.2						
	non-univ.	35.0	34.7	34.5							
	overall	40.2	40.8	41.3							
Germany	univ. level	28.8					34.5	34.0	34.6	34.8	34.8
	non-univ.	5.4					14.8	16.1	19.3	21.4	21.6
	overall	23.6					30.7	30.1	31.7	32.3	32.1
Italy	univ. level	32.5	34.0	35.2	36.0	37.2	38.2	36.9	37.7	—	—
	non-univ.	46.1	47.7	48.2	49.9	48.2	49.4	48.5	—	—	—
	overall	32.9	34.4	35.6	36.4	37.4	38.5	37.2	—	—	—
Netherlands	univ. level	18.0	18.3	18.5	18.6	19.1	19.7	20.7	—	—	23.1
	non-univ.	30.4	31.4	32.5	33.4	33.7	34.0	34.1	35.9	35.9	36.6
	overall	25.2	25.7	26.4	27.0	27.2	27.5	28.0	—	—	30.8
UK	univ. level	25.2	25.6	25.9	26.2	26.5	27.2	28.0	28.8	29.9	—
	non-univ.		34.6	36.3	37.7	39.6	39.6	40.2	40.9	41.6	—
	overall		30.2	31.2	31.9	32.8	33.2	33.7	34.4	35.3	—

Source: Hecquet et Verniers, *op. cit.*, Tableaux de synthèse.

in enrolments at the start of the 1970s (9). Indeed, in certain countries, only the increased numbers of women entrants prevented a marked fall off in the overall number of students enrolled. Such was the case, for example in the United Kingdom in both the university and non-university type courses, amongst university level courses in Belgium and the Netherlands and amongst the non-university levels of study in Yugoslavia where the number of men enrolling tended to remain steady (10).

Discussion

In this chapter we have looked at various indicators as well as the trends that result from them within the context of the development of systems of higher education in some of the EEC countries. The general picture that emerges from 1967 / 8 onwards is one of a marked slow down in the expansion of higher education. This was foreseen only very partly by studies conducted by the OECD some years ago, studies which took as their base indicator demographic trends and the size of the relevant age cohorts. In fact, the fall in the rate of expansion has proved more abrupt than almost any previous projections intimated. To what extent this has influenced the policies of various governments we will examine later in the course of this study. Generally speaking, with the exception of Germany, most countries have found themselves faced with a coincidence of crises — these crises arising first, by a flattening out of the proportion of school leavers qualified to enter higher education and second, amongst those qualified, a reluctance to continue on with higher education.

In the absence of any cross national empirical studies in this domain, it is, of course, extremely difficult to provide any explanation other than the obvious one of the fear bred by the prospect of graduate unemployment, a fear particularly rife in the early 70s. One should, however, admit that this is not necessarily the only explanation, nor the most valid. Recent figures on enrolments seem to suggest that prolonged economic recession forces school leavers back into higher education as a refuge from the ranks of unemployed youth.

What we do not know is the manner in which this fear might or might not have altered the decision making process of individuals at the point of leaving secondary school for higher education. The simple economic explanation, though satisfactory to some extent, does not provide, still less take into account the subtleties involved in, an explanation based on a sociological perspective. We do not know at present to what extent structural change in secondary schools, the creation of a 'universal' system of secondary education for instance, might have affected this issue.

There is, however, good reason for thinking that policies involving structural transformation at the secondary level are not without major importance, first, within the general context of equality of educational opportunity; second, on account of their very specific effects upon the articulation of higher and secondary education.

As regards the first point, it is worthwhile dwelling a little longer on this aspect since it illuminates some of the problems thrown up for higher education by operating a policy of educational opportunity at the secondary level.

That policies of equalizing opportunity in education are carried out in both secondary and higher education simultaneously does not mean they complement one another or that they are mutually supporting. Indeed, the way such policies are implemented in the secondary school can create fundamental dilemmas for institutes of higher education supposedly endorsing a similar programme.

In the secondary sector, the basic element in equalizing educational opportunity involves the 'universalization' of secondary education, or in less abstract terms, the emergence of a system of comprehensive secondary schools for the whole of the secondary sector. The consequences of this can be said to be two fold: first, the admission of a more diverse range of aptitude, ability, background and interest in the 16 to 19 age range; second, the opening up, potentially at least, of a more diverse clientele for post-secondary and higher education. The major implication then is to create a far more complex system of decision making at that stage of the education system. This complexity can emerge in a number of ways — curricular, in the form of new school leaving certificates and new subject tracks — structural, in the way in which students of varying abilities are grouped together for purposes of teaching and learning; or, ultimately, personal, as a result of creating more complex structures which in turn demand a more complex decision making process by individual students.

This development stands in marked contrast with those historic and traditional patterns of differentiation between schools of an 'academic' nature whose pupils are, by dint of attending them, thought to represent the future pool of ability destined for university, and those schools whose pupils are destined for early insertion at the lower levels of the labour force.

On a curricular level there is already strong evidence, in Sweden, Denmark and to a lesser extent in France and Germany as well, that new routes of access through new school leaving certificates are opening up (11). But the fact of opening up potential access to higher education to groups which, hitherto, were excluded from that possibility, also involves increasing the pool of students whose decision making is marginal to the question of continuing on to higher education. Indeed, a diversity at the post-16 stage of secondary education implies that the task of the school is not necessarily and certainly not uniquely to concentrate upon getting all students at that stage in the education system to higher education. It is to cater for all ranges of ability and for all ranges of career intention. What is often not recognized in the establishment of 'universal secondary education' or 'open structure schools' is that they permit, by their very nature, greater flexibility not only in the curricular domain, but also as a logical extension of that, flexibility also in the domain of personal decision making. And that, in turn, involves the breaking down in the hitherto accepted historical and paternal task of the academic school — namely the conditioning by which it is automatically assumed that all students reaching a certain point in the education system are *ipso facto*, part of the 'higher education pool'.

Taken within a broader context for a moment what this implies, though one must admit that this can be viewed only theoretically since no studies have yet been undertaken on a wide enough basis to make it a general proposition — is that external and environmental influences, those of an economic order, of the family and of the peer group, are probably of greater import in the 'open structure' school than they are in the closed world of the 'academic school'. In short, the universalization of secondary education appears to create either an instability of choice or, looked at from a positive standpoint, greater pupil flexibility in decision making which in turn, runs, temporarily at least, counter to projections and planning which assume either a stability of pupil behaviour as regards higher education or, by the same token, an inflexibility in individual decision making.

Nevertheless, the slowing down in the expansion rate of higher education is far from being a pointer to the failure of policies which endorsed a notion of growth eternal. Indeed, the contrary is the case. The greater the demand for higher education, the less responsive institutions of higher education are to the demands for either curricular reform or for more flexibility in entry conditions. What this means, in effect is, as simple as it is astounding. Only in times of unfilled vacancies is it possible to introduce policies of equalizing educational opportunity to higher education. In times of high demand, institutes of higher education can effectively, subordinate the curriculum of the school to their 'requirements'. In times of relatively restricted demand, the relationship between school and higher education is reversed. Only at this particular conjuncture is it possible for higher education institutes to admit the possibility of finding alternative routes of access, routes which bring into higher education those groups, who, by dint of being placed on them in secondary education, would hitherto have been excluded from post-school learning. In other words, if the 'open structure' school has the possibility of introducing new flexibility in pupil decision making, it also forces higher education to endorse, albeit in most cases reluctantly, a similar flexibility and thus a similar policy — namely, the further development of educational opportunity.

Since this conjuncture is only partly in the control of governments — governments may for instance, legislate for both secondary and higher education, they cannot, however, completely control the behaviour of individuals — such an interaction constitutes one of the most powerful forces for change. How governments have responded to this situation, or have adjusted their plans in the light of some of the developments described in the course of this chapter, we will examine in the course of the next.

Chapter 3

Planning and Policies for Structural Innovation: an Overview

In the last chapter we examined some of the patterns of quantitative development in higher education in various selected States in Europe including those in the EEC. Generally speaking, the picture that emerged was one of a slowing down in growth rates, but, as a result of the expansion that took place during the previous decade, access to higher education had become far more widespread. The questions upon which we hope to cast some light in this chapter are two: first, what are the general planning trends upon which various Western governments, including some in the EEC have based their educational strategy for the ensuing years up to 1980? Second, what — if any — are the various types of structural innovation envisaged within the framework of higher education?

Not all governments will, of necessity, have been forced to rethink their forward planning in terms of structural transformation, that is, in terms of creating new patterns of institution in the post-secondary sector. Nor, for that matter, is the information necessarily available for all countries in respect of forward trends and projections. Consequently, this chapter is not an exhaustive review. It does not for instance, include those countries where structural change plays no part in future educational strategy — for example, Italy. It does not include those countries whose major reforms concentrate on secondary education, for example Belgium.

There is a further observation that needs must be made. It is highly unlikely that individual countries employ similar mechanisms of planning. Hence, the way one may envisage its future is not necessarily compatible with the methods used by another. Bearing in mind these strictures, this chapter will, accordingly present a country by country resumé of the main considerations prompting forward planning in higher education followed in each case by the various proposals for structural innovation.

A. The German Federal Republic
1. *Forward planning trends*

In Germany, planning in the area of demand for university places has been carried forward to 1978. Over the five years from 1973 to 1978, the number of students in higher education will — it is estimated — increase by some 35 per cent, reaching 813,960 (12). It is envisaged that demand for places — that is the excess number of students over the places available — will diminish in the university sector as well as in arts and sports colleges. It will, however, rise in the specialized colleges. In consequence, the number of students per place available will be some 49 per cent in excess of building programmes for this area, by 1978.

As far as the *Fachhochschulen* are concerned, demand for places will considerably exceed supply. The subjects where the greatest pressure will occur are design — with 2.27 applicants per place compared with 1.13 in 1973 — and natural sciences, 2.09 in 1978 compared with an excess of places in 1973.

Reading between the lines, one gets the impression that higher education planning in Germany faces a situation analogous to that of Britain in the late 1960s when the original Robbins' estimates were exceeded by a wide margin and subsequently called forth hasty revision upward in all quarters (13). According to the overall education plan by 1980, 22 per cent of the 19 to under-21 age group will be provided university places (14). Present trends predict that this figure will be reached in the current year — 1975 — if applications were continued unchecked. By 1980, the estimated number of applicants is thought to represent 27.1 per cent of the relevant age cohort.

2. *Proposals for structural innovation*

With planning well in hand, the first German version of the Open University, situated at Hagen (Nord Rhein Westphalia) has taken in its first students. Unlike its British equivalent, it is not a national structure but local, operating out of 18 study centres across the Land. The Hagen University for 'Distance Study' will work as an independent entity with its own staff and students. It is reckoned that the first intake will be in the region of some 9,000 students who will follow a three or four year course. Two thousand of them will embark on a mathematics course, of four years duration. The remainder will begin in economics which will last between three or four years. Amongst other courses to be developed are two in biology and psychology. One of the main advantages of this innovation is, as has been noted in connexion with the British Open University, the considerable saving in the cost of teaching per student. Distance teaching, carried out by means of correspondence courses, cassettes and radio programmes, will reduce the per student cost by about two-thirds compared with the 'traditional' university. A major difference between Hagen and Milton Keynes — and we shall come back to this later — occurs in the access conditions. The Open University in Britain is, as its name implies, open to all, on a first come, first served basis (15). Hagen, by contrast, demands the traditional qualifications associated with university entrance, that is, the possession of the *Abitur*.

B. The Netherlands
1. *Forward planning trends*

The Netherlands government has carried out studies into the demand for higher education up to 1990. Even when every attempt has been made to avoid overestimating the number of students coming from middle and higher secondary education, the general conclusion remains that the growth of students in higher education casts serious doubts on the ability of society in the 1980s and 1990s to absorb so many (16). Two methods were used to estimate future demand for graduate manpower for the next 15 years. The first involved a follow up of graduates into employment and their distribution amongst different sectors of the labour market and the economy. This was related to such factors as productivity and the size of the firm into which they passed. The second was a differential approach, viewed from the standpoint of the demand for graduates amongst various sectors of the economy and the type of occupation offered by the civil service, health and education. These structural factors were subsequently examined in relation to the type of course graduates had followed. Both approaches, however, yielded substantially similar results (17). The general prognosis suggests that society is moving towards a situation in which degrees no longer guarantee automatically a position in society. However, the possession of a degree is, for the same reason, becoming more crucial for entry into the world of work.

The area where pressure for places at university is particularly developed are veterinary science — 3.2 applicants per place in 1975 / 6 — and medicine 2.2 applicants per place (18). By contrast, there would appear to be some 'slack' in the domain of technical sciences.

The conclusion reached by the Netherlands planning authorities suggests that an increase in the number of students in higher education may no longer be desirable either from the standpoint of the labour market or from the standpoint of the current 'socioeconomic situation'. (19)

2. *Proposals for structural innovation*

The major reform of higher education in the Netherlands involves not so much institutional restructuring as the curtailment of the length of courses in the 12 Dutch universities. The proposal, originally presented by the late Professor K. Posthumus has been approved by the Lower Chamber of the Dutch Parliament. It is almost certain that the Bill will pass into legislation soon and take effect from September 1978.

The essence of the proposals does not differ very greatly from the Danish reform (*vide infra*, p. 45). In place of courses lasting up to 10 years in some cases, all areas of study will be reduced to four years, composed of an initial year for a propaedeutic examination and three years bringing the student up to the level of the *doctoraalexamen*. Failure in the propaedeutic year will mean a student cannot continue to the *doctoraalexamen*, though one resit is allowed. Should a student fail at the end of the three year period following admission to the doctoral programme, he may attempt to pass the examination again the following year. As with the propaedeutic year, only two attempts to pass the final examination are permitted. Hence, the normal period of study will be reduced to four or five years, depending on the type of programme a student embarks upon, with the possibility of seven years if individuals should fail both examinations.

Universities will be asked to present an evaluation of their experiences with propaedeutic studies in 1981 with a similar report with regard to the *doctoraalexamen* in 1984. On the basis of these reports, the Minister of Education will consider whether the new system should be continued or not.

C. Norway
1. *Forward Planning trends*

The situation in Norway stands in marked contrast with the two previous countries we have examined. In the first place, the Norwegian authorities estimate that the annual growth rate in the number of students enrolled in university type institutions will be in the order of two per cent. In the second place, there seems little difficulty in balancing the supply of graduates with the demands of the economy and the labour force (20). Unemployment in general has been very low, which has tended to minimize the difficulties recent graduates face in finding a position in their chosen field of specialization.

As in most European countries the employment of graduates is most difficult in the case of social science and humanities specialists. In Norway the former do not appear to have met with any major difficulties as yet, whilst the latter face a rather more unstable situation, depending on whether the secondary education system can take them on as teachers (21). Generally speaking, ' . . . the unemployment problem has, in absolute terms been trivial.'

To some extent, the policy of competitive entry to almost all Norwegian institutes of higher education may be seen as a primitive regulator mechanism. The *numerus clausus* is wielded in faculties of medical sciences and technology and, in a limited fashion, similar strictures are now being placed on the humanities, physical and natural sciences, faculties that, hitherto, have been open. In the non-university sector, applicants far outnumber the places available. In 1972 and 1973 for example, only 54 per cent and 55 per cent of applicants in those two years were admitted (22). The effect, somewhat paradoxically, is to make entry to the district colleges far more difficult than entry to the university.

2. *Proposals for structural innovation*
Structural innovation revolves around the development of the 2 year district colleges. Since this is one of our target institutions to be examined in more detail in the course of this study, we will omit any discussion of it here.

D. The United Kingdom
1. *Forward planning trends*
In the United Kingdom, projections for the future development of higher education are based on the principle of private demand enunciated in 1963 by the Robbins Committee. Demand is calculated on the basis of school numbers, numbers of 'qualified' school leavers, entrants to and places available in higher education. In previous sections we have seen the degree of 'slow down' in the rate of expansion in the UK higher education system (23). This has imposed a revision on government forecasts. In 1972, the estimated number of students in higher education by 1981 was reckoned to be 750,000. By 1974, this projection has been reduced to 640,000 (24).

The official explanation of this cutback is, first, that the number of school leavers qualifying for higher education are slowing down. This in turn is the result of a slowing down in the proportion of the group remaining in secondary school after the school leaving age. A second factor appears to be the growing reluctance of qualified school leavers to enter higher education. This self denying ordinance presents somewhat of a puzzle. Numerous explanations can be presented for it, some of an economic order, others of a more sociological and psychological nature. But research within the Scottish framework suggests that it acts differentially and that the reluctance to apply to university is most marked amongst working class students and those with qualifications on the 'borderline' of the 'going rate' (25).

Turning to the question of the labour market, it appears that the situation in the United Kingdom is not dissimilar in this regard to that pertaining in the Netherlands. The general outlook for 1981 is one in which a certain degree of 'graduate saturation' can be expected. In a suitably sybilline utterance the Department of Employment's Manpower Unit suggested (26) that, assuming a total of 700,000 students in higher education by 1981 'between one and four per cent of men graduates and between 18 and 22 per cent of women graduates might be employed in jobs not *traditionally* (our italics) filled by graduates' (27). This of course, begs the question as to whether the 'traditional' jobs have in fact been replaced by the development of new industries, or whether with the occupation structure remaining constant, 'non-traditional jobs' are deemed to be those well below the skill level of those in which graduates are currently employed.

2. *Proposals for structural innovation*

The main area of structural innovation in the United Kingdom is represented by first, the Open University and second, by the polytechnics, institutions which are to be investigated in depth in this report. In consequence, we will leave the discussion of them until later.

If, however, we expand the field of our interest from institutional to pedagogic structures, one highly significant development in the latter group has been the introduction of the Diploma of Higher Education. The Diploma of Higher Education was originally outlined in the White Paper of 1973 *Teacher Education and Training*, which summarized the cogitations of the Committee chaired by Lord James of Rusholme. It proposed a two year course, relatively flexible with a 'general' and a 'special subject' base. The Diploma of Higher Education was seen not only as a terminal qualification for those wishing to enter the teaching profession, but also as a step towards training for other occupations as well. Hence, provision is made for the possibility of transfer either to university level or CNAA degree courses after the basic two years have been completed. Normal entry qualifications for students wishing to embark on this Diploma are reckoned to be two Advanced Level subjects in the General Certificate of Education though there is the possibility of exemptions from this stipulation if the applicant holds equivalent certificates.

The Diploma of Higher Education is therefore a highly flexible instrument which, depending on resources available in those institutions — so far relatively few — where it has been introduced, allow both a wide area of subject choice and study mode.

Current research into the development of this qualification remains, however, somewhat sparse. Suffice it then that we note the potential significance of this development and leave to some later investigation the task of ascertaining whether the intentions correspond to the reality.

E. Denmark
1. *Forward planning trends*
(detailed information not available)

2. *Proposals for structural innovation*
The main considerations involving the reform of higher education in Denmark are mainly questions of access. Higher education in Denmark has expanded extremely quickly over the past 12 years. In 1960, 13 per cent of the age group embarked on higher study and 28 per cent in 1972 / 3. Current estimates reckon that by 1975 this will reach 32 per cent and perhaps go as high as 40 per cent by 1978. One of the most powerful reasons for restricting the intake to long course study is the high 'drop out' rate — around 50 per cent for arts and humanities students and approximately one student in five following engineering or natural sciences.

The reform proposes to introduce a one year propaedeutic programme on the basis of performance in which the decision to admit a student to long course study, who should go to a short study or who should quit will be taken. The general tenor of the intended reform suggests that its main task is to reduce the number of students starting upon long course studies. The realization of this programme depends in no small degree on the possibility of students having enough leeway or flexibility to change courses and to re-orient themselves into those areas of study which present maximum economic usefulness when they leave. Such flexibility is possible only in institutions having a diversity of study levels. Hence, it is suggested that university centres should be set up, preferably where there is an existing graduate school but also comprising various colleges and schools for training in such areas as nursing and social work. The university centre, comprising both theoretical and vocational studies, those of a long and a short course, of a general and specialized nature, is an attempt to create a multiple access model of higher education within s single institutional type. This 'multi-access' model not only offers students the possibility of great diversification but also should, it is felt, allow them to meet the situation — however it evolves — in the graduate labour market (28). The University Centre at Roskilde may perhaps be regarded as the shape of things to come.

F. Republic of Ireland
1. *Forward planning trends*
(detailed information not available)

2. *Proposals for structural innovation*
Earlier this year, a spokesman for the Irish Ministry of Education

announced that proposals were being considered for the creation of a 'comprehensive' system of higher education. In the main, the plan under discussion appears to involve bringing into the university sector certain colleges, particularly colleges of technology, which previously occupied a position outwith the university ambit. The intention of the Irish authorities is to incorporate top ranking colleges into the university sector and to provide them with the power of conferring degrees. The Minister stressed that this was not the same policy as the British 'binary system' of coexisting universities and polytechnics. Rather it should be seen as a coalescence of two systems, both in the interests 'of the students and of society in general' (29). In addition, such an arrangement has the not inconsiderable advantage of avoiding duplication of resources.

It should in fact be noted that this policy bears considerable resemblance to an earlier stage of development in the British university system towards the end of the 1950s and the start of the 1960s. During that period, a considerable number of colleges of advanced technology were promoted to the status of technological universities; for example Bradford, Salford, the City University and Aston in Birmingham (30).

G. France
1. *Forward planning trends*
No information available at time of writing this report.

2. *Proposals for structural innovation*
Current proposals for reform in the French system of higher education do not, strictly speaking, involve structural innovation in the sense of creating new institutional patterns. Rather they involve changes of a curricular nature, particularly in the second cycle of university studies and also the reform of the teacher training system. As regards the first, the Secrétariat d'Etat aux Universités proposed altering the pattern of studies following on from the *Diplôme d'Etudes Universitaires Générales* (DEUG). By the start of the academic year 1977, this will consist of two levels: the first, will be oriented around fundamental elements of a particular field of study or fields of study, with the second forming a master's year (*année de maîtrise*) more specialized and leading more directly to a particular profession. The general tenor of this proposal is to give greater credibility for such degrees *vis à vis* future employers. Not all DEUG's will be valid for admission to second cycle studies, however. The conditions for entry will set out for each particular field or discipline.

The second area of reform involves teacher training. Hitherto, teaching training for secondary schools in France has been undertaken by the universities on the one hand and the Inspectorate on the other.

Whilst the former taught the theoretical aspect of teaching training, the Inspectorate had the role of evaluating the results. It has been suggested that current needs in secondary education demand a different approach involving both a vocational and educational pedagogic expertise. The Minister for Education stated in October that whilst he was happy to have the universities collaborate in this new proposal, he did not intend that they should have the total responsibility for teacher education. The development of professional expertise in the teaching domain should, it is proposed, be organized by the educational administration on the grounds that universities have relatively little knowledge of the requirements and demands in this area.

As for the structural changes in French higher education, perhaps the most significant is the evolution of the IUTs which, since they figure in this study we will leave until later.

Discussion

In this chapter we have reviewed the forward trends in some European countries, most of which are members of the Common Market. In three of them — Germany, the Netherlands and the United Kingdom — there is a considerable degree of consensus about the major problem of the next half decade or so. It is the problem of graduate un- or under-employment. Allied to this is a theme which is familiar to any educational planner and administrator: how to forecaste with reasonable accuracy the likely demand five years hence and thus to be able to plan to meet it with a judicious and equitable policy programme? The answer to this problem has not been found. In times of rising demand, forward extrapolations have shown themselves woefully inclined towards underestimating it. And in times of decline, of underestimating its extent as well. In short, not enough is known of the way in which individuals think about, perceive and act through, the situation they regard as pertinent to them. Indeed, the unpredictable nature of the effects upon the higher education system of the present industrial crisis seems to find additional evidence in the recent enrolment figures. Although provisional, these suggest an upturn in the number of entrants to university. Again, how far this might be due to the realization amongst school leavers that the unemployment rate is lower for holders of university degrees and other types of diplomas from higher education than for those provided merely with a school leaving certificate must remain unknown — at least for the present.

Yet, there is evidence also, albeit of a demographic nature, that would explain this recent phenomenon, namely the size of the age cohort. In most European countries, with the exception of Western Germany, the late 60s was a time of a fall in the size of the age group from which higher education drew its students. Taking the year 1970 as its reference point, a recent study has shown that by 1980, the size of the age cohort will have increased by a third in Great Britain, by around eight per cent in the Netherlands, by 10 per cent in Italy, by six per cent in Belgium and about two per cent in France. In Germany, the peak will be reached only in 1985, when the age cohort will be some 35 per cent larger than in 1970 (31). In other words, for the demographic increase *not* to have the effect of increasing the growth rate in higher education would require a massive move of qualified young people from applying for places in higher education, or failing to reach the standard required for entry.

If the present relative slump in the growth rate of higher education gives way to a new boom, regardless of its causes, then without a doubt it will strengthen government's intentions *vis a vis* the introduction of the *numerus clausus*. Indeed, if one considers carefully the motives behind the thinking that inspired structural innovation, it seems to be how to cope with the spiraling costs of higher education and, at the same time, bring education closer to the perceived needs of the economy. With the possible exception of the Irish Republic, where the motives behind the proposals for a 'comprehensive' system of higher education remain somewhat unclear, both the Dutch and the Danish reforms, for instance, have as their overriding priority to reduce the length of studies or, alternatively, to dissuade large numbers of students from entering long course study. Given the economic blizzard, this is a comprehensible attitude to take. However, it is perhaps not out of place to suggest that, if such are the main motives, then educational policies in a time of monetary inflation consist in aspirational deflation!

There is, however, another perspective from which one can view these recent developments; namely, that they represent the belated passage of education systems which, at the higher levels at least, have hitherto evolved within the confines of 'traditional structures'. Obviously, if the second stage of post-war development in higher education began in 1966 in both England and France, there is absolutely no reason why it should not take place earlier in some countries — which is the case of Yugoslavia — and later in others. Seen from this angle, both the Dutch and Danish as well as the Irish proposals are merely part of a protracted process by which education and the economy are inevitably and inexorably bound together. Hence, such proposals represent the passage of those countries into the second stage of post-war development in higher education.

Part Two

The Growth of New Structures
in
Higher Education

Chapter 4

The Place of New Structures in Higher Education

Introduction

In selecting the institutions which may be regarded as coterminous with structural innovation in higher education, we have used no other criterion than the fact that, in varying degrees, they represent interesting and perhaps, significant departures from what might intuitively be termed 'normality' in higher education. Since structural innovation is not limited to EEC countries we have included two institutions — the district college in Norway and the *vise skole* in Yugoslavia (two-year post-secondary college) — outside the Community. Nor have we confined ouselves to the non-university sector, though it has to be admitted that a good deal of pioneering work in this area happens to coincide with institutions that do not enjoy university status. Hence, those included in this study are not homogeneous. Most fall into the non-university sector, one represents an attempt to integrate post-secondary education into a coordinated whole — the *Gesamthochschule* Kassel — whilst the Open University represents perhaps the most radical attempt to overthrow structural and qualificatory barriers that, hitherto, have surrounded the traditional university.

If most of the major innovations in structure are, in one form or another, included in this report, one should however, be cautious in claiming that our choice of institutions is representative of any notional 'population'. They stand as examples, differing in type, purpose, goals and strategy from which we may, hopefully find some general themes which illustrate some of the problems, difficulties, successes and failures associated with attempts to realize some measure of equality of educational opportunity. Nevertheless, this begs the question somewhat. Though these institutions might be contributing significantly to equalizing educational opportunity, that does not mean to say that such was the original intent of the governments which called them into being. If such *was* their purpose, then by examining their progress since their foundation we can see to what extent this purpose has been fulfilled. By the same token, if educational opportunity was *not* the main consideration then we can see perhaps, what the main causes of this educational 'spin off' were. Either way, we need to know the objectives assigned to our target institutions at their inception and also their particular administrative relationship *vis a vis* the universities in their respective countries. The latter is necessary. It arises out of the particular methodology to be employed in this study which will consist in the main of comparing the structures, goals and achievements of each of these institutions against similar trends and developments in the 'classical' university. In short, the university is, in each case, our norm of reference.

A. Instituts Universitaires de Technologie

By 1973, 58 *Instituts Universitaires de Technologie* (IUTs) have been established in France. The geographic location of these institutes was planned to provide higher education for those areas which, hitherto, remained bereft of a university. The number of IUTs per academic region (*académie*) varies considerably. For instance, the Rennes academic region has five and that of Nantes four. However, the location of these establishments is to some extent determined by demographic considerations. Hence, it is not surprising to find a particular concentration in such 'university' towns as Paris (8 IUTs), Bordeaux, Nancy, Grenoble, Lyon, and Lille (2 each).

Most of the courses and degrees offered in the IUTs show a highly vocational and practical element, with a particular emphasis on the applied sciences. Amongst the latter one finds applied biology, chemistry, civil, chemical and electronic engineering, mechanical and thermal engineering. The vocational element is provided in other areas with such studies as information careers, social work training, business administration, computing, statistics and quantitative methods for business administration.

As originally conceived, the *Instituts Universitaires de Technologie* were to provide specialized training for higher technicians in the secondary and tertiary sector of the national economy. Furthermore the IUTs were seen as providing training methods (*fonctions nouvelles d'encadrement technique*) in areas between pure research, upper administration and the actual manufacturing process. Such training, it was stated, involved a higher degree of specialization than normally afforded to engineers, a more general education than that given to technicians and an overall ability to adapt to constant change and development in industry, commerce or administration. Created in the first place as a university institute, they occupied a position that was parallel but outside the traditional university system (*Decree of January 7th, 1966*). In short, a situation not dissimilar to that of the polytechnics. From a standpoint of administrative practice this system had two precendents: first, the decree of 31st July 1920 which attributed the role of meeting new requirements in higher education to specific university institutes: second, the creation of the *Ecoles Nationales Supérieures d'Ingénieurs*. The policy consisted in the main in setting up a second university system, independent from the traditional university, but more flexible in operation (22). The legal and structural reform of the university sector following May 1968 saw a change in the relationship of the new IUTs. This involved a closer integration of the IUTs within the new university structure, but, at the same time maintained them under a closer degree of state control a procedure intended in part to prevent their total assimilation into the university and in part to maintain their particular educational role. *Vis a vis* the university, such an arrangement gives the IUTs a certain degree of administrative autonomy. At the same time it also places them under a different administrative regime, such that their finance depends largely on the central government and the Ministry of Education in particular. The universities, by contrast, are financed through the intermediary of a university area (*université*) to which a general grant is made by the central government. It is then distributed amongst the component institutions (*Unités d'Enseignement et de Recherches, UERs*) within the particular locality.

B. Gesamthochschule Kassel

The creation of the *Gesamthochschule* Kassel should be seen as part of a wider programme currently being undertaken in the German Federal Republic with a view to setting up regional educational networks. These 'networks' will, it is hoped, bring together hitherto dispersed and separate institutions – universities, *Fachhochschulen* and teacher training colleges – under one organizational umbrella. This might be said to be a certain vision of the 'comprehensive university'. At the time of writing, this programme is in the evaluative stage. Five experimental institutions exist, for instance, in Nord Rhine-Westphalia in the towns of Duisburg, Paderborn, Siegen, Wuppertal and Essen. In addition there is one in Bavaria at Bamberg and one in Hesse at Kassel.

In theory, the process of development from a separate to an integrated model of higher education involves three distinct phases. The first involves the setting up of closer links between bodies previously autonomous. This stage of the reform corresponds very closely to what one might term a multilateral pattern of institution, or, to borrow an expression current in German secondary education, the establishment of an *additive Gesamthochschule*. Effectively, it amounts to an administrative reform in which academic and vocational higher education are brought together in one organization without necessarily uniting the respective student bodies around a common or shared curriculum. The second phase in the evolution of the comprehensive university can be seen as an elaboration of the administrative development so far implemented. It revolves, in the main, around the creation of joint liaison committees between the participating institutions whilst, at the same time, still maintaining their legal independence. Only during the third and final stage does the new pedagogic transformation take place. This involves the setting up of common educational programmes and thus lays down the basis of an integrated university, or, if one returns to the secondary sector parlance, the *Integrierte Gesamthochschule*.

The particular significance of the *Gesamthochschule* Kassel lies in the fact that, of the seven institutions for which such development is envisaged, it is the only one so far to have gone beyond the phases of development. Obviously, Kassel, founded in June 1970 (33), has a considerable way to go. Based on an engineering university, an agricultural school, a school of fine art and a teacher training institute, its major priority falls into the area of curricular innovation and the creation of new patterns of study to bring together students who, otherwise, would have followed widely different courses and to bring them together on a common level. At the present time, its concern is less with providing alternative methods of access though the fact of having united various component institutions into one body means, *de facto*, that this is the case. Nor, in a formal sense it is engaged on policies which one would commonly identify with creating equality in educational opportunity (34). This is not to say that such a consideration lies outwith its ambit. Rather its concern lies with breaking down those qualificatory barriers that exist at the entry to various professions. For the *Gesamthochschule* Kassel, then, equality of educational opportunity is determined less by the conditions of access at the point of transfer from secondary to post-secondary education, but rather at the point of entry into the world of work after graduation.

C. Norwegian district colleges

From January 1st, 1976, the district colleges, first established on an experimental basis in 1969, will become permanent institutions. Their original task was to provide a means of evaluating the effects of diversification in higher education as the first, though not necessarily the final step to this overall objective. At present, seven colleges are functioning, with plans for a further 10 to open over the next few years. Each college will be located in an educational district and act as the focal point for integrating all non-university post-secondary education into a single unit. Once this change has been carried out, it is envisaged that the colleges, hitherto known as district colleges, will be termed study centres around which will be grouped teacher training institutes, schools for social workers and engineering schools (35).

The main task of the study centres follows on from that which was attributed to the earlier experimental district colleges. This was to meet the increased demand for higher education and also to encourage decentralization. The obverse of this particular coin might also be regarded as meeting the educational requirements of particular geographic areas — an aspect which, previously, had been neglected by the university sector.

Financial responsibility for the new district colleges is assumed by the government which determines, in consequence the expenditure of the various component institutes gathered around the study centre. Ultimately, it is envisaged that executive power for the administration of the district colleges will be transferred to a regional board from the central authority. The board will reflect the links between education and the community and hopefully stimulate greater local involvement in this new type of institution, by having local politicians as a majority of its members.

In contrast to the French model, however, the district colleges are in process of developing linkages in two directions — on the one hand with the university and on the other with non-university institutes, for instance, teacher training, social workers and engineering schools. This is as much evident in the type of study offered as it is in the possibility of transfer from the district colleges to university and *vice versa*. The new institutions will include a combination of basic university courses together with two year vocational studies. In some respects therefore, they show certain similarities with the Yugoslavian *vise skole* (*q.v.*) during the earlier phase of their development. Students taking university level courses will have the possibility of transfer thanks to a system of credit transfer points (36).

D. The British Open University

The first intake of students entered the Open University in 1971. Currently it has some 49,000 students on its books. The organization of the OU is extremely complex. Physically, it is based on a central administrative headquarters at Milton Keynes, a town some 50 miles northwest from London. This nerve centre groups several hundred teaching and administrative staff, data processing equipment and wide ranging materials for the creation and distribution of course material. It has, however, no students.

In order to cope with an extensive home study programme, the OU has divided the United Kingdom up into 13 administrative regions. Each region, regarded as semi-autonomous, has its own director and regional head office together with its own academic and administrative officers. Its main role is a coordinating one and involves organizing all the Open University's activities in its particular area. These comprise such matters as tutorials, counselling, controlling the various study centres etc. The study centres, of which there are approximately 300, are designed to bring students together and to put them in contact with part time tutors and counsellors.

The academic organization involves a division into six faculties, arts, social science, mathematics and science, technology and educational studies. Study programmes are based on a 'Foundation Year' pattern.

Like most British institutions of higher education, the Open University does not have a legally defined purpose, other than the normal charter granted to establishments attaining university status. Indeed, it has been argued that the Open University shares in the original sin of its venerable colleagues by having extremely vague basic objectives (37). These may be discerned to some extent from official documents or discussion papers but also from its organization. Its main role, stated in the 1969 Report of the Open University Planning Committee, was to offer higher education to 'those who for one reason or another have not been able to take advantage of higher education'. This was conceived in terms less of post-experience but rather as undergraduate studies (38). As a chartered university, it is an autonomous body, but with this difference. University finance is usually negotiated in the form of a quinquennial grant with the University Grants Commission acting as intermediary between the universities on the one side and the Treasury on the other. This arrangement is thought to preserve overdue government interference in the running of independent institutions and also to be more flexible than the quinquennial grant system during the early years of the OU's operation. The Open University, by contrast, is financed through the Department of Education and Science. It should perhaps be stressed at this junction that from an organizational standpoint, the Open University is less a university in the sense of physically grouping students to follow courses in one particular location. It is, rather an education *system* in its own right. Furthermore, with a high degree of standardization and control over its outlying centres, it presents the somewhat bizarre spectacle of being a *centralized* system of learning in a country where traditionally all areas of education secondary, primary, further and higher are administered on a decentralized basis.

E. The English and Welsh Polytechnics

First proposed in the White Paper of 1966, *A Plan for Polytechnics and other Colleges*, there are now 30 institutes of this type in the UK. Polytechnics are to be found in major centres of population, some in towns where a university already exists — for example, London where there are five, Manchester and Leicester. Equally, however, they are also to be found in non-university towns as in the case of Portsmouth, Sunderland and Wolverhampton. The size of polytechnics is particularly difficult to estimate. Much depends on how one calculates part-time and sandwich course students, the latter being those who, released from industry, follow a course for six months before returning for a certain period to industry and subsequently, reverting to the polytechnics to fulfil the remainder of their course. It is probably correct to say that the average number of students, regardless of whether they are full or part-time, is in the region of 3,500 per establishment.

The type of studies undertaken in such institutions is extremely diverse, ranging from technical diplomas of a non-university degree level to post-graduate and doctoral studies. It is also very eclectic in the curricular content which can range as far afield as applied sciences, technology studies on the one hand, to combined arts cum social studies on the other. One of the more interesting features of the polytechnics is their attempt to create cross disciplinary courses which, whilst providing a general education base, also correspond to what is felt to be the needs of industry; for example, the combination of business studies with languages, or economics with an emphasis on one particular European country.

A close perusal of the relevant government documents shows that the main purpose in creating the binary system was to bring higher education into line with the provisions of the National Plan which forecast the need for some 70,000 full time and 'sandwich' students following advanced courses in institutions of higher education (39). The main aim in setting up the polytechnics was, first, logistic — that is, to meet the number of places deemed necessary; second, to concentrate full time education in a 'limited number of major centres in which a wider range of both full time and part-time courses can be developed' (40). Amongst other intentions mentioned in the course of the main planning document were the forging of mutually advantageous links with universities 'through the sharing of staff . . . and other facilities' (41).

The polytechnics, as the term binary implies, are independent of the universities, governed under a different status and financed through a system of central and local government grants as well as through an advanced further education pooling of grants. Legally speaking, they are responsible to the local education authority of their locality,

though, in instances where the polytechnic has been formed as a result
of merging several colleges of further education or technical colleges,
this is replaced by a Joint Education Committee formed from the
authorities previously responsible for the constituent colleges. The
difference between the method of resource allocation and accoun-
tability to local authorities is perhaps the major administrative
distinction between the universities and the polytechnics (42).

In theory, the type of education polytechnics offer is deemed to be
more professionally and vocationally biased than universities though
equally specialized. Strictly speaking, they are not 'new structures'. The
historical origins of the polytechnics and the type of education they
offer go back to the end of the last century. Nor is the diversity in the
type of courses they purvey especially new either. Sandwich courses,
for instance, existed in the Colleges of Advanced Technology in the
1950s (43). And part-time courses have long been the feature of the
further education system in the UK.

F. The Yugoslavian vise skole

Similar to the Norwegian regional colleges, both as regards their
priorities *vis a vis* the local community and their relationship with the
university, the *vise skole* conform to what has been termed a
'multi-purpose model' of post-secondary education (44). Information
on the exact number of *vise skole* (two year post-secondary schools) is
not available from the sources at our disposal. Nevertheless, it is
apparent that these institutions have brought about a considerable
dispersion in the geographic location of centres of post-secondary study
mainly as a result of allowing the various local communities the
possibility of setting up their own establishment. The main areas of
study included in this institution are teacher training, which accounts
for around 30 per cent of the student intake, economics which is taken
by one quarter of all enrolled students and technical education, which
accounts for approximately a fifth.

The development of these two year post-secondary schools followed
the passing of the Resolution on Technical Personnel Training and
Education in 1960. The main intention behind the setting up of these
new institutions was to meet certain changes in the economy which
suggested a need for skills on an intermediary level between the
theoretical and the practical aspects of production. Requirements such
as those for intermediary grade technicians and personnel, social
services anticipated by some six years the motives that set up the IUTs
in France. They did not, however, lead to the same pattern of structure
in the two year post-secondary schools, which provide a two to three
year training. This could either be taken as a terminal degree or diploma
or, as an alternative could be presented as the first level for a university

course (45). The importance of this arrangement was two fold: firstly, from a long term standpoint, it would have provided a practical basis of study, grounded in current economic requirements even for those students who, later, continued on to university. Secondly, from a curricular standpoint, it would have provided a means of integrating 'academic' and technical education, for those who later would have entered major managerial and administrative positions in society. In some respects, however, the original intentions did not work out. Adjustments in the curriculum at university level were not always satisfactory. Some universities adopted the 2 + 2 model. Others did not. Indeed, recently, there appears to have been considerable backsliding by universities which have rapidly abandoned these first level courses. In part, the very partial success of the 2 + 2 model of post-secondary education in Yugoslavia was not simply a function of the reluctance of universities, but also of industry to provide the new pattern of graduates from the two year post-secondary schools with jobs commensurate with their training (46).

From a legislative standpoint, the most important change that the introduction of the two year post-secondary schools brought about was the decentralization of higher education. The Resolution on Technical Personnel transferred the authority to set up institutions of higher education from the federal government to the various provinces and republics. Nor did decentralization stop there. It could, if necessary, be transferred to even smaller decision making units, to the communes for instance. Such a step was fully in accord with the basic objective of the reform, namely to democratize higher education, firstly, by making it accessible to social groups hitherto excluded and, secondly, and also as a means so to do, to permit close development in conjunction with local industries and social service organizations. In fine, like the Norwegian reform, it involved the redistribution and, where possible, the equalization, of the graduate labour force throughout the country.

Discussion

In this section we have examined firstly, the main considerations which, from an official point of view, prompted the setting up of new structures in higher education. Secondly, we have paid particular attention to the relationship of the new structures with the 'traditional' university sector and also to the legislation that defined this relationship, at the outset of the reform. In some cases, as for instance, with the IUTs, subsequent legislation has modified this relationship. In others, for instance, the *vise skole*, the relationship has undergone subsequent change which is not, however, reflected in official promulgations or decrees. The degree to which official legislation modifies the original intentions and relationship with the university, of the new structures is, of course a reflection of the degree of centralized control in a particular education system. Indeed, the greater the decentralization, the more likely that any subsequent modification in objectives will escape official sanction, simply because modification is carried out either within the institution itself, or by authorities and personalities who do not occupy official positions in the original decision making body. We shall examine this aspect of change when we come to investigate the criteria of equality implicit in the various institutions of each country.

From a functional point of view, it is apparent that a major feature, common to many of the new structures in this study involves the physical dispersion of higher education. Perhaps the most significant feature to have emerged from our investigation so far is what one might term the 'dispersion of higher education'. We have seen, for instance, that some IUTs in France are located in areas which, hitherto, lacked institutions of higher education. We have noted too that the notion of bringing higher education to the regions was an explicit goal of the *vise skole* in Yugoslavia and also of the district colleges in Norway. Indeed, the physical organization of the Open University stands as a most important example of the principle of dispersion.

Dispersion does not necessarily entail change in hitherto existing administrative relationships, though obviously, it can do so, as we have seen, for example, in Norway and Yugoslavia. Here, physical dispersion involves administrative decentralization. In France, however, we have a contrary model in which physical dispersion is still built upon a high degree of central control. In some respects, this is true also of the Open University. For, although autonomous as a university, and although physically dispersed, its central organization maintains a high degree of control over its outlying parts. In fine, central control in the case of this latter institution is ensured, not through legislative means so much as by curricular.

The significance of this trend should not, however, be underestimated. For in effect the development of higher education over the past century in Europe has tended to place universities in particular centres where political, administrative and industrial power coincided. In other words, the concentration of financial capital which made possible the industrial revolution was followed by a concentration of intellectual capital. Indeed, fortunes made in industry were very often devoted to creating universities in precisely those towns where the fortunes were themselves created. Hence, the trend we see in the case of the new structures has as an implicit goal the breaking down of this historic monopoly over post-school learning. Equally important is the explicit belief that regional development depends, at least in part, upon the more equitable distribution of places in higher education amongst a country's various regions.

Taking a wider view for a moment, one finds interesting parallels in certain developments which took place in the United States during the Post Bellum period. There, far earlier than in Europe, the concept of regional development was seen in terms of structural innovation in higher education. The setting up of the Land Grant Colleges not only laid down the basis of the egalitarian tradition in American higher education, but by the same token, broke the historic monopoly, hitherto unchallenged, of the elite status East Coast universities, founded in the Colonial Era. Indeed, the parallelism becomes even more striking when one considers that the Land Grant College was conceived, like many of the new structures today, as providing a pattern of education in keeping not merely with the skills required in their areas, but a pattern of education designed for mass consumption.

Chapter 5

Problems of Equality

Introduction
When we talk about 'equality of educational opportunity' we are not talking about an 'objective' value-free phenomenon (47). Contained in this apparently similar expression are a whole host of different ideologies which, because they hold an implicit concept of models of society, are essentially of a political or of a social nature. Thus, educational opportunity is defined in relation to the type of society one would like to see — either preserved or developed in the near, alternatively, in the far distant future — depending on one's personal beliefs. In opting for a particular interpretation of educational opportunity we are then, opting for certain social practices and elaborating a programme of action which amounts to a political act in the broadest meaning of the term. Whatever their historical or philosophical origins and whatever their interpretation of Man's original state, ideologies share one point in common — namely, a belief in the educability of human beings. The degree to which they are educable and under what optimum circumstances, is, of course, subject to intense and often bitter controversy. But regardless of the extent to which it is believed that human beings are more or less educable and capable of benefitting from education, such beliefs influence one's personal convictions as to how society *ought* to be run or, as an extension of this, how education *ought* to function. Between the policy recommendation and the moral imperative the line is very narrow and easily overstepped.

Nowhere is the frontier between policy and belief more ill-defined than in education. Thus it is scarcely surprising that recently a number of challenges have been levelled against those policies designed to realize 'greater equality of opportunity'. Critics such as Christopher Jencks have, for instance, pointed to the apparent impotence of educational policies to realize this particular end (48). 'Economic success', he wrote, 'seems to depend on varieties of luck and on the job competence that are only moderately related to family background, schooling or scores on standardized tests'.

Hence, programmes intended to facilitate greater access to education are not, themselves, likely to achieve their goal. To a certain extent, this argument found support, though of a more general nature, in a recent report published by the *Organisation of Economic Cooperation and Development*. 'Big increases in education in the 1950s and 1960s, it concluded, brought about only marginal advances in equality of opportunity' (49). It is perhaps, fair to point out, however, that we do not know how far greater inequality would have resulted from *not* implementing policies to equalize educational opportunity during that period.

Allied to the current economic problem, attitudes towards equal opportunity programmes seem to tend towards a more pessimistic interpretation compared to the interpretation and importance attached to this policy during the previous decade. Optimism and expansion and change have given place to pessimism, contraction and a certain degree of judiciously chosen scepticism. Yet, regardless of whether one endorses the pessimistic or the optimistic premise of equality in educational opportunity it is certain that many reputations have been won and lost in trying to sort out the philosophic principles behind the concept. Suffice it then that we take as axiomatic that equality of educational opportunity has a relativistic nature, and that we go on to identify some of the ways in which it might be operationalized. Yet, even the act of operationalization is itself value implicit. In choosing our indicators, our choice is dictated by a certain covert stance which may be cast into one of three possible ideal-types. These are:

1. the Elitist interpretation;
2. the Socially oriented interpretation;
3. the Individual centred interpretation.

At this point, one should perhaps emphasize that the following typologies represent a personal analysis of the phenomenon that may, to some appear as standing apart from what has been seen as a normal mode of presentation. Basically, however, each of the three categories places a different weighting upon various structural features in education systems from the other two. This in turn affects the way in which individuals subscribing to a particular ideal type will choose to define equality of educational opportunity. And, from this it follows that, depending on the priorities implied or chosen by each group, so the way in which the performance and assessment of education systems will alter. Hence, it is important to identify the manner in which those subscribing to each of our three value-interpretations will define equality of educational opportunity and thus the types of variables they would choose for their evaluations.

Definitions of educational opportunity

1. *The élitist interpretation of educational opportunity*

Axiomatic to the elitist interpretation of educational opportunity is the belief that:

a) intelligence is innate;
b) intelligence can be objectively measured by psychometrical testing;
c) past a certain stage of development one can predict the level of intelligence of the adolescent and the adult on the basis of his or her performance in verbal and mathematical reasoning tests taken in early puberty or slightly before.

Within these parameters, equality consists in the right of all children judged 'able' in the light of these procedures and regardless of their social origin, to pursue studies to the highest level without financial hindrance. In effect, educational 'opportunity' is restricted — notionally at least — to a certain top per cent of the ability range. The structural concomitants of this belief are the following:

1) that the point at which equality is determined in the education system takes place at the juncture of primary with secondary schooling;
2) that secondary education consists of a series of 'filtering' or screening devices, in the form of either of successive examinations or of internal 'tracking' systems in the school, winnowing out the less 'able' from the 'able';
3) that the purpose of such schools is social mobility and through a policy of 'educational Darwinism' to feed into elite occupations through the university nexus;
4) that education is a sequential process such that the passage of a sixth former, *Abiturienden* or *élève de première* to higher education is direct;
5) that the success of an education system is judged by the quality and attainment of those students entering university.

2. *The socially-oriented interpretation of educational opportunity*

The socially-oriented interpretation of educational opportunity, though differing in its basic premises about the nature of intelligence, nevertheless incorporates certain features particularly with regard to the structural patterns of the education system from the elitist definition.

The fundamental premises of the socially-oriented interpretation are:

a) that intelligence is influenced by 'private environment' e.g. home, family, parental expectations;
b) that intelligence can be measured but that it is subject to change within the individual depending on his personal circumstances;
c) that, in consequence, one cannot determine an individual's potential, except over a long period.

Equality, as defined by these guidelines, consists in educating all children through similar programmes, with a certain degree of compensatory education for the environmentally disadvantaged at the secondary level. The structural consequences of the socially-oriented interpretation are:

1) that the point in the education system at which differentiation begins is curricular, namely, when certain pupils are prevented from sitting particular subjects at the end of a common 'core' usually around 14 years of age;
2) that secondary education still consists of a series of filtering or screening devices, but the period during which a pupil can gain qualifications is prolonged;
3) that the purpose of schools is not necessarily social mobility, but the creation of a 'cooperative society' by overcoming the structural divisions that have perpetuated divisions of social classes;
4) that education is a sequential process from secondary to higher education, but, due to the policy of delaying selection in the 'middle school', hitherto disadvantaged groups in society may have a better chance of access to post-secondary and higher education;
5) that the success of an education system is judged by the proportion of pupils remaining in school, after the statutory leaving age.

3. *The individual-centred interpretation*

Just as the socially-oriented interpretation shares certain premises in common with the elitist, so the individual-centred interpretation shares certain basic credos with the socially-oriented. Its main distinguishing feature, however, is to be seen in the purposes it assigns to higher education. Using the same system of analysis we find that the individual-centred interpretation endorses the following notions:

a) that intelligence is influenced by both private and public environment, the latter being the relationship of the individual's family to the means of production;
b) that intelligence is a cultural phenomenon and cannot, therefore be measured in any way that is meaningful;
c) that an individual's potential depends on the creation of a suitable

environment in the education system in response to his needs as they develop.

Within such a framework, educational opportunity is not measured in terms of examination passes, nor in terms of sheer numbers of pupils reaching a given point in the education system, but in terms of the possibility of the individual to make use of and have access to, the means of knowledge. Hence, we find the following differences in the structures of an education system which, in theory at least, would respond to these criteria:

1) though the school system might differentiate between individuals on the basis of their ability, this distinction does not have permanent consequences in excluding them from access to education at a future date. Hence, the lacunae of secondary education can, later, be overcome by access at all times to post-secondary education.
2) that the secondary school as far as possible is free from filtering mechanisms. The bulk of its task consists in positive discrimination in favour of socially disadvantaged groups: emigrants, dwellers in twilight zones, those below the national minimum wage or on its borderline;
3) that the school is a means or a vehicle for social reform outside presently existing social and economic structures;
4) that education is not a sequential process, but may be taken up whenever the individual perceives the need;
5) that the success of an education system is judged by the degree to which it can provide for the multiple and diverse needs of all classes and all individuals.

The discerning will perceive that these three 'political' models or definitions of equality of educational opportunity may be equated roughly with the two post-war periods of development in higher education. However, the elitist definition for example can just as well operate in times of expansion as it can in times of steady state development. Indeed, within this context, the Robbins Report may, essentially, be regarded as espousing the élitist interpretation. In essence, its justification for expanding British universities rested on the concept of the 'reserves of talent' that emerged from a highly selective secondary education system. The socially oriented interpretation may be seen, therefore as coterminous with the second stage one that is our particular concern given that it sets up most of the 'new structures' in higher education. The individual centred interpretation, though still in a state of elaboration in most Western European countries, is equivalent to the notion of *education permanente* and as such, may be seen taking shape in Sweden. Recent figures for entrants to Swedish universities have shown a remarkable increase in the number of older entrants with work experience (47).

It should be said, *en passant*, that few education systems will conform exactly and completely to any of the three models proposed here. Many will share certain traits or characteristics. On the other hand, a system endorsing a particular definition or operating in support of any of the three definitions outlined, will have a tendency for the majority of its features to be in one particular category. This merely reflects the fact that, in varying degrees, education systems, both at secondary and post-secondary level, are moving away from the élite model and, in varying degrees, making the transition to the socially-oriented or the individual-centred definition.

Operational characteristics

This brings us to the question of the operationalization of such definitions. Since we are concerned only with higher education, we will examine this in terms of possible characteristics found first, in methods of access and second, in terms of the educational and social background of the student body, at university.

1. *Élitist*

A) Access: this is governed by certain 'tracks' or combinations of subjects, which, at secondary level, predict to a high degree those who will or those who will not enter university. Failure to hold the appropriate combination of subjects or to be on the 'right track' results in a quasi-total exclusion of the student. *Viz*: filiere C Technical studies in France, relevant A-level combination in the UK, i.e. a single route of access to university study.

B) Student characteristics: predomination of one particular type of school (since access to higher education in conservative systems limited often to a school giving 'academic' education *viz*: lycée, gymnasium, public school, grammar school). Direct passage from school to university. Full time study, long course, degree level.

2. *Socially-oriented*

A) Access: multiple 'track' access to long course study in which different qualifications at an equivalent level are recognized as valid. For example, possession of OND as qualifying for degree level study in the United Kingdom, or the *omnivalence des diplômes* in Belgium.

B) Student characteristics: greater diversity of school type background. Direct passage from school to university. Predominance of full time study, though some students enrolled in part-time or sandwich courses.

3. Individual-centred

A) Access: multiple 'track' access to long course study in which different qualifications at varying levels are recognized as valid. Institution provides 'compensatory' courses for students not officially endowed with formal qualifications necessary for the course of study they envisage. e.g. Open University introductory courses.

B) Student characteristics: greater age spread of first time entrants. Reduction in the proportion of direct entrants from school. Diversity of study modes, full-time, part-time, sandwich. Diversity of study levels. Diversity of study time (drop in, drop out system).

Having described the various operational characteristics that may be found in educational systems subscribing to the various patterns of educational opportunity, we will, in the next chapter, examine to what extent the new structures – IUTs, polytechnics, Open University, regional colleges – correspond to these models.

Chapter 6

The New Structures and their Conditions of Access

Introduction

In the previous chapter we discussed the concept of 'equality of educational opportunity' in terms of three ideal-types. We also suggested certain criteria which, depending on the model one chooses, would enable an evaluation of the ways in which education systems might be said to fulfill or move towards 'educational opportunity'. In this chapter, however, we are faced with less philosophic considerations. Briefly stated, its main thrust is to examine to what extent the new structures may be said to endorse either one — or any — of the categories we set out previously.

There are two ways in which one may assess and evaluate this aspect. The first involves an analysis of the official legislation governing policies of admission. The second is to analyse the degree to which the student body of these same institutions has — if at all — subsequently altered either with respect to admissions criteria or with respect to the situation pertaining in the universities of each country. The purpose in examining official legislation is simply to see to what extent the government, ministry or controlling agency, permitted in a formal manner, the admission by other 'routes' of students who otherwise might have been excluded. To the extent that such a strategy is permitted, then one can say that the notion of 'compensatory educational strategies' were incorporated into the original purpose of the particular institution. Yet, official legislation does not necessarily tell us all there is to know about the extent to which new structures might operate policies for greater educational opportunity. Institutions have their own internal dynamics. Over time, they manage to build up practices and methods of working which, regardless of the reasons for their existence, can often go far beyond what was originally intended by the legislator. As we pointed out at the end of Chapter 1, this may be said to introduce a certain amount of institutional flexibility, always necessary if, faced with changing and unforeseen circumstances, the institution is to comply with the spirit of its foundation rather than with the rigid adherence to intent which might no longer be relevant.

This second — and unofficial — dimension to the evolution of new structures is certainly as relevant to the question of equality of educational opportunity as the formal articles of government. Hence, this chapter will fall into two main parts. The first will deal with the official legislation governing conditions of access to our target institutions. It will also allow us to establish them in relation to the three 'models' of educational opportunity outlined previously. The second will deal with the place occupied by the new structures within the higher education systems of their respective countries. It will be statistically based on the main.

In Chapter 4, we examined the administrative relationship between the new structures and the 'classical' university. To some extent also, we touched upon the general objectives and purposes that lay behind their establishment. In the case of Norway, Yugoslavia and the Open University, there was a specific objective which corresponded to equalizing education opportunity. In the case of the IUTs and the polytechnics this was not a formal goal. Rather the major priority was one of curricular reform, the creation of new patterns of courses with a view to providing and meeting current manpower planning needs. It is important to realize that responding to industrial and commercial demands for a certain type of specialized manpower does not have to be the same as opening up higher education to hitherto underrepresented social and educational groups. One can just as well meet the demands of the economy by diverting those groups who would, in any case, have continued to higher education and in particular to the university, to other areas of study, for instance, more vocationally relevant disciplines. Hence, the policy of structural diversification does not, of itself, represent a move towards the socially-oriented interpretation of educational opportunity, still less to the individual-centred one. It can just as well be implemented within the framework of a policy whose interpretation of equality remains firmly anchored in the élitist tradition.

Conditions of access to the 'new structures'
A. *The Instituts Universitaires de Technologie*

The conditions of access to the French IUTs are somewhat paradoxical. Whilst the university is open, insofar as all holding the baccalaureat may enter, the IUTs operate a policy of selection. Under the terms of the legislation governing entry conditions, the 'baccalaureat is neither necessary nor sufficient' (50). The decree governing admission — that of 7th January 1966 — specified three ways in which students could enter these Institutes. First, if the applicant was studying for a *Brevet de Technicien Supérieur*. Students in this position had, in the early stages, a priority since the development of the IUTs involved closing down the *sections de techniciens* (51). Second, applications can be made to an admissions committee headed by the rector of the academic region (*académie*) which then decides on the basis of an application form (*dossier d'admission*). This includes reports on the applicant's progress during the last three years of school (52). Such a route of access is usually taken by holders of the baccalaureat. Third, there is a method of entry by examination. In this case, the decision resides with a jury. Students using this method are those who have failed the Baccalaureat. However, the terms of the legislation stipulate they must have reached at least 8 / 20 in the formal school leaving examination.

A number of objections have been made *vis a vis* this system, not the least telling of which is that it amounts to a *numerus clausus*. Given the structure and organization of the IUT, which is based on departments of not more than 150 students, the function of the admissions committee is, therefore, to limit successful applicants to this number (53).

This apparent legislative rigour in fact covers a considerable diversity of practices. Obviously, the degree to which selection is − or alternatively, is not − stringent depends on the number of applicants. And the number of applicants is itself subject to variation depending on the type of department the student wishes to enter and also on the particular locality of the IUT. Given these variations then, it is possible that a high degree of selection for one department in one IUT is not met by a similar policy elsewhere. There is, then, the real possibility that certain institutions and certain departments do not operate a policy of selection at all. Like engineering faculties in British universities, all who wish to enter, can.

Given these stipulations, how in theory could the IUTs meet the challenge of equality of educational opportunity? And, in meeting it, what 'model' would it conform to? As with any education system, regardless of the prevalent ideology, the extent to which particular institutions can tip the scales from one model to another depends on the initial social demand. That is, if the population of applicants is biased towards particular social groups, then by dint of selecting from that population one does not necessarily fulfil an active role in forwarding educational opportunity. Yet the fact that, for example, such an institution might attract large numbers of hitherto underrepresented social groups in higher education, is indicative of its institutional effect. In theory, given the strict conditions of entry it may be possible for admissions panels to admit groups whose qualifications — or lack of them — would otherwise have excluded them entirely from higher education. On this point alone, it is arguable that the IUTs represent, theoretically, the passage from the *elitist* to the socially orientated interpolation of educational opportunity.

B. *Gesamthochschule Kassel*

As we have indicated earlier, the status of this institution is still relatively fluid. It is regarded as an experimental establishment and thus, like Mahomet's coffin floating between Heaven and Earth, is seeking to carry out innovation within the legislative boundaries promulgated *vis a vis* earlier patterns of higher education. Conditions of access are still dictated by the regimes of the component institutes which have been welded into an integrated whole. These are, on the one side, the classical university and, on the other, the *Fachhochschulen* (higher vocational colleges). Successful entry to such establishments requires the possession of the *Abitur* or the *Fachhochschulreife* (higher vocational college certificate) respectively. Effectively, then the institution itself has no lattitude in which it may overcome or dispense candidates from these requirements. In other words, the degree to which equality of educational opportunity might be achieved in this institution is subject almost entirely to social demand, and also to the degree to which the Universities Central Clearing agency assigns students to it from out state areas. Hence, the *Gesamthochschule* depends on a different concept of educational opportunity from the normal. It does not see this task as involving the admittance of otherwise unqualified groups, so much as contributing to the opening up of the occupational structure at the top through curricular reform and through the creation of new study areas. Since the German education system is founded upon rigid differentiation of pupils at age 12, the present model to which the *Gesamthochschule* responds is the élitist one.

C. *The district colleges*

Apart from the objectives already enunciated in Chapter 4, the explicit task of the regional colleges falls into three groups: first, the societal, second, the pedagogic and third, the individual's personal development. More specifically, its role as far as it involves equalizing educational opportunity will be achieved through increasing the interaction between higher education and society by developing alternative study modes through part-time and recurrent education; by stimulating reforms in other sectors of the education system; and by stimulating the development of the student's personality and critical faculties instead of merely hawking knowledge (54). Despite the fact that admission to these colleges is selective, the objectives are clearly within the boundaries of the individual centred interpretation of educational opportunity.

D. *The Open University*

Admission to the Open University depends neither on the possession of prior qualifications nor on the decision of an admission committee. There are certain limitations on the number admitted, and to some extent therefore a certain degree of *numerus clausus* exists. Ultimately, however, the decision rests with the individual applicant. An explicit objective of the Open University is to cater for '. . . those who left at an early stage (so that) they would have an added incentive to equip themselves by such means for higher study' (55). By dint of having an 'open door' admissions policy, though how far this is successful often depends on the degree of knowledge that individuals have of the opportunities this presents (56) and by dint of being a non-sequential institution the Open University falls fully into the individual-centred interpretation of educational opportunity.

E. *The polytechnics*

Given the wide diversity of courses in polytechnics — part-time, full-time, sandwich — and the varying differences in level — degree and sub-degree level — there are no uniform conditions of entry to these institutions. To what extent therefore, prior qualification *is* a condition of entry and what the precise qualifications are that are required depends on the particular course. Generally speaking admission requirements are not controlled by the polytechnics so much as by the professional bodies or national associations for which the course prepares students: OND, and ONC or in the case of degree courses, the Council for National Academic Awards. Formally, at least, this places control over the degree to which the polytechnics can actively engage in a policy of compensatory education in the hands of external bodies. Though to what extent this can be bypassed in reality is a question we shall examine in the course of this chapter.

How far such institutions can realize a greater degree of equality of educational opportunity is difficult to assess from official legislation. The major documents devoted to this sector of British higher education are concerned more with administrative considerations — resource allocation, efficient usage of existing plant — than with the explicit task of creating greater equality of access to higher education (57). Indeed, the interpretations of the polytechnics' role — and thus their contribution to equality of educational opportunity — are as diverse and conflicting as one would expect from individuals presenting personal opinions. On the one hand, they have been presented as vehicles whose major and imperative task is to give a second chance to those groups in society underrepresented in university (58). On the other, they have been seen as predominantly an institution 'to minimize the differences between the education and training required by industry, commerce and the education, skills and knowledge that people have' (59). At a general level, then, given the diversity of courses and levels of study, one can say that the polytechnics correspond to a transition from the socially-oriented towards the individual centred interpretation of educational opportunity.

F. *The vise skole*

The conditions of access to the *vise skole* are changing. The New Higher Education Law assumes that everyone so wishing can complete his or her secondary education. Thus, only holders of secondary school leaving certificates will be admitted to institutes of post-secondary education (60). Up to the present, however, entry to the *vise skole* could be realized through three specific routes. The first consisted in being a high school graduate from a 'corresponding' or 'adequate' secondary school, a system not dissimilar to the New Zealand pattern of accredited schools. Students not from recognized schools could gain admission by sitting an entrance examination and satisfying the admissions board. A third route, destined mainly for working people who left school early, stipulates that they should be 18 years or over, have completed an eight year elementary school and have a certain degree of working experience. Applicants in this position sit an examination for the particular course they intend to pursue (61). There is no distinction made between the entry demands for part-time study and those for full-time. Indeed, the major work of the *vise skole* is the provision of part-time study and the education of those currently employed. Though in theory, these institutions are open to the whole of the economically active population, the fact that they have a limited set of entry conditions limits the extent to which they can provide 'compensatory' education at the higher level. This is perhaps less important in a country where the degree of differentiation between different types of schools — between for instance, grammar and secondary technical schools — has less drastic effect upon the life chances of students placed in either one or the other. Nevertheless, it is obviously not so far reaching in its entrance conditions as the Open University, for example. Hence, the model of educational opportunity to which it corresponds can be said to lie athwart the socially-oriented and the individual-centred models, since the presence of large numbers of part-timers demonstrates that access to higher education is not necessarily sequential as in the 'true' socially-oriented model.

Having looked at the various entry conditions of our target institutions we have found that, theoretically at least, largely different interpretations of the concept of educational opportunity are implicit in the criterion of their entry conditions. If we group them on a scale going from the élitist to the individual centred interpretation we find they occupy the following positions:

Diagram 6.1: Location of various new structures according to the interpretation of equality of educational opportunity implied by their entry conditions

---

Elitist	*Socially Oriented*	*Individual Centred*
Gesamthochschule Kassel		District Colleges
	Vise Skole	
IUT		Open University
	Polytechnics	

However, before we can examine in detail the extent to which the 'new structures' have — or alternatively have not — contributed towards the equalization of educational opportunity we need to know the position they occupy inside their respective education systems, particularly their numerical strength. This is important not merely from an informational point of view, but also because the number of students in the new structures as a proportion of all students in higher education is a factor that largely decides how far they are actually contributing to this objective in a systematic sense. At this point we should, perhaps make a distinction between the 'systematic contribution' of new structures and their 'potential or latent contribution'. By 'systematic contribution', we mean how far access to higher education as measured by the social class background of the student body has improved throughout higher education over a given period. The systematic contribution is therefore the total picture of the social class background of students from the university and from the new structures combined. However, in cases where the new structures form a comparatively small proportion of the total number of students in higher education, obviously, whatever difference there is between the social origins for students in university and those in the new structures will not affect the overall class composition of higher education to a very great extent. In such a situation, for example, the contribution of 'new structures' towards the equalization of educational opportunity depends on their expansion. We shall hope to show therefore at what point in the evolution of

Table 6.2: Development of the new structures compared with the development of higher education overall in France, the United Kingdom, Norway and Yugoslavia, 1966 to 1973

Country	Institut		1966	1967	1968	1969	1970	1971	1972	1973
France	IUT	Higher Education[1]	71.3	77.2	87.1	100.0	105.5	109.4	116.3	122.2
		N=				736.060				
		New Structures[2]		13.8	44.9	100.0	144.9	204.4	296.6	349.5
		N=				11.927				
		% 2 of 1		0.3		1.6				4.4
United Kingdom	Polys	Higher Education	76.7	85.2	94.0	100.0	102.8	106.2	108.9	110.6
		N=				564.000				
		New Structures	—	—	—	100.0	350.7	396.5	387.8	373.5
		N=				41.076				
		% 2 of 1				7.3				24.6
United Kingdom	Open Univ.	Higher Education								
		New Structures						24.220	37.396	42.639
		% 2 of 1								
Norway	District Colleges	Higher Education			87.7	100.0	109.8	119.6	128.9	
		N=				27.483				
		New Structures								
		% 2 of 1								
Yugoslavia	Vise Skole	Higher Education	79.9	84.4	91.1	100.0	103.6	112.9	122.1	130.4
		N=				231.444				
		New Structures	81.8	89.6	98.4	100.0	92.8	96.9	106.7	109.0
		N=				83.947				
		% 2 of 1	37.1			36.3				30.3

higher education the potential contribution of our target institutions *would* affect a change in the overall social class background of entrants to higher education.

Position of new structures in higher education (enrolment figures)

In order to show the relative importance of the new structures in their respective countries we have calculated the overall enrolment of students in higher education between 1966 and 1973. The year 1969 has been taken as baseline simply because all our target institutions, with the exception of the Open University, were functioning, albeit fitfully at that date. Three items of information are given for each country. The first is the overall rate of expansion in higher education. The second is the rate of expansion in the 'new structures'. The third, represents the total enrolment of students in the 'new structures' by year as a percentage of all higher education enrolments in the country concerned. This information is presented in Table 6.2.

From Table 6.2 we see that the position of the various new structures varies greatly from country to country. Some form a major part of the total higher education system, catering for large numbers of students. Others form a relatively small proportion of the total enrolments. We see for instance, that the *vise skole* in 1966 catered for just under four students out of ten in the whole higher education system in Yugoslavia. In subsequent years, this role has become less important. By 1972 / 3 just over one student in three enrolled in such institutions. The reason for this decline, as we pointed out in Chapter 2, derives from the greater drive of entrants into the university sector over the last few years, a trend that is generally counter to that found in most other Western European countries.

In France, by contrast, the *Instituts Universitaires de Technologie*, represent only a small fraction of total enrolments in higher education, around one student in twenty-five in 1972 / 3, a figure well under the target proposed for the current four year plan which envisaged some 10 per cent of all enrolments in the IUTs by that time. To some extent, the relatively minor role of the new structures in Norway and France stems from their relative recent foundation and, probably more influential, from the fact that the creation involves the mobilizing of considerable financial support involved in any foundation beginning *ab initio*. By contrast, the English polytechnics enrolled one student out of twelve in 1969, a figure which rose to one out of four in higher education overall by 1972 / 3. The rapid growth of the polytechnics is, however, due to particular circumstances: first, their creation involved the upgrading of certain already existing colleges of regional technology or regional technical colleges; second, the government made explicit in its policy that any further expansion in higher education would take place in polytechnics rather than in universities. This policy was endorsed by both Labour and Conservative parties alike, indeed reinforced by the latter administration in the White Paper: *The Expansion of Higher Education*, published in 1972.

Given that rates of growth are largely reflections of government policy in this area, it would be somewhat crass to judge whether an institution was successful or not simply on the basis of the proportion of students in higher education it succeeded in attracting, especially since such a calculation fails to take into account the fact that designated polytechnics already possessed a substantial student body from their days as technical colleges.

However, from the picture that emerges from Table 6.2, it is evident that, even assuming the new structures already to have introduced a certain measure of equality of educational opportunity compared with their university colleagues, it will have a very varied impact upon the total system of higher education.

Summary

In this chapter we have examined the formal entry conditions to our various target institutions and in their light, grouped them according to the degree to which the institutions correspond to our tripartite model of educational opportunity. We also examined the statistical importance of the various new structures within the general context of their particular systems of higher education. This, we found, was extremely varied, going from one student in twenty-five in the French IUTs to four students in ten enrolled in the English polytechnics.

Chapter 7

Changes in the Composition of the Student Body

Introduction

This chapter consists of an institute by institute analysis of the degree to which our new structures are — or alternatively, are not — contributing to equalizing educational opportunity by comparison with the more traditional university model in each country. Two base variables are normally associated with assessing the impact of educational models upon equality of opportunity. These are first, the social class origins of their student entrants; second, their educational background and history.

Though most major reports on educational policy (for example, *The Plowden Report, The Jencks Report* in the USA) take for granted that social class is an important indicator of the disequilibrium in education systems, it has been argued — and persuasively — that social class by itself constitutes what one might term a sociological short hand. Class, though a powerful predictor of the degree to which individuals are able or unable to manipulate and take advantage of, education systems is not the most powerful one. And moreover, though it might predict, it does not, of itself *explain* why children from a given class should be in a better position to benefit from formal education and teaching (62). Far more potent are those attitudes, home environment, parental expectation, membership of anti-school peer groups and subcultures which, whilst themselves highly correlated with social class, are nevertheless present in each and every social grouping, albeit in varying degrees. Hence, if one seeks an explanation for the apparent failure of certain groups in society to take advantage of the facilities presented them by the education system, class is a less predictive variable than the possession of these psychological and environmentally induced traits, which are transcendant of class, though at the same time highly correlated with it.

What this suggests is that, if one adheres merely to the routine measurements of equality based upon social class differences, one is not necessarily examining its whole dimension. Rather one is concentrating on one particular manifestation. Thus, to use social class as an indicator, however convenient and easy it is to gather in national statistics, is to endorse only a *minimum* programme for combating inequality. Essentially, then, by using the variable social class as a vehicle for assessment in this study, we are merely showing the degree to which our various institutions are moving towards equality of opportunity in its *minimal* state.

Changes in participation in higher education amongst various social classes 1960—1970

Generally speaking the past decade saw a considerable improvement in the participation of students from working class backgrounds in higher education throughout the West. This is shown in Table 7.1 which uses the same technique as that employed by the OECD study on Participation in Higher Education (63). Obviously, different countries have differing occupational structures and varying methods of defining what constitutes membership of a given social group. The OECD study cited above sought to create a cross-national system of occupational classification that would permit meaningful comparisons between countries. The system utilized in the Participation Study involved a five part occupational grouping, in which A corresponded to the upper social stratum, B to the middle stratum, C represented independent agriculturalists, D other independently employed and E the lower stratum, that latter representing the group coterminous with the industrial working classes.

Table 7.1 also shows the extent to which the monopoly of upper class entrants in higher education has, over the decade of the 1960s gradually been reduced, though it still remains by far and away the most important single numerical grouping in all higher education systems with the exception of Germany and Yugoslavia. Against this background, we can now proceed to examine on a country by country basis the contribution of the new structures towards the equalization of educational opportunity.

Characteristics of student bodies
A. *France: Instituts Universitaires de Technologie*

In our examination of the ideological dimensions of equality of educational opportunity and the extent to which our target institutions corresponded to one of the three interpretations, we suggested that the IUTs represented a transitional stage from the élite to the socially oriented interpretation. The common characteristic of both 'ideologies'

Table 7.1: Social class background of students in higher education by country

Country	Year	A	B		C	D	E	Others
			Social Class group					
England +	1961	61.0	13.0		–	–	26.0	–
Wales	1970	46.0	27.0		–	–	27.0	–
France	1960	55.2	34.4		5.8	–	4.6	–
	1968	47.0	30.7		6.3	–	11.9	–
	1974*	42.5	39.2		6.4	–	11.9	–
Germany	1961	34.2	29.0		3.6	14.7	5.4	–
	1970	26.2	35.7		4.2	14.3	12.6	–
	1972**	24.7	34.4		5.9	19.7	12.5	2.3
Netherlands	1961	42.0	––– 47.0		–––	–	8.5	–
	1970	37.0	––– 49.0		–––	–	14.0	–
Norway	1964	33.6	11.1		12.0	–	23.9	–
	1970	37.6	11.0		7.5	–	19.5	–
	1971***	40.2	13.0		8.6	–	21.5	16.6
Yugoslavia	1960	––– 40.1	–––		26.5	–	17.5	3.0
	1970	21.5	28.8		20.2	–	20.5	9.4

Sources: J.P. Pellegrin, 'Quantitative trends in post secondary education 1960–1970', in *Towards Mass Higher Education, issues and dilemmas*, Paris, OCDE, 1974.
* Secrétariat d'Etat aux Universités. *Les Caractéristiques de la croissance des effectifs universitaires d'après l'origine sociale des etudiants de 1960 à 1974*, Paris, 1975, p. 37.
** *Bevolkerung u. Kultur Reihe 10V Studenten u Hochschulen: Wintersemester 1971 / 2*, Stuttgart u. Mainz, 1973 Kohlhammer, pp. 92–3.
*** NOS *Undervisningsstatistiskk Universitaeter og Høgskoler*, Fall 1971, Oslo, 1972, pp. 129

Table 7.2: The social class background of students from IUTs and universities in France in 1967 / 8 and 1973 / 4 compared with the total class composition of the French population in 1970 / 1

Social Class	1967 / 68		Popula-tion 1964 / 5	1973 / 74		Popula-tion 1970 / 1
	Univ. %	IUT%	%	Univ. %	IUT%	%
Agriculturalists + agric. labourers	6.6	11.9	21.2	6.4	12.8	17.4
Industrialists	14.7	15.1	11.3	11.9	12.4	9.4
Liberal professions	33.2	11.8	5.0	23.6	14.7	5.2
Cadres moyens	16.6	16.5	5.7	16.3	15.1	6.3
Employees	9.0	–	6.7	9.4	9.9	7.6
Workers	10.5	21.6	37.7	11.8	23.7	40.1
Services personnel + undetermined	9.4	23.1	13.4	9.8	11.4	14.0

Source: Ministère de l'Education Nationale, *Etudes et Documents n⁰ 31*, Paris, 1975, p. 56, Table xxxiii.

is their dependence on well defined entry conditions, without which entry is not possible. In other words, in this ideology, such institutions are built upon the structural inequalities of secondary education. They do not offer any 'compensatory' role by admitting relatively unqualified students, although, legally, we saw that some degree of latitude remained to the selection committees for admission. French writers on the IUTs have stressed two aspects in which they might contribute to equalizing educational opportunities: first, since IUTs are short cycle institutions, hopefully they would attract in particular students 'from social groups with financial handicaps' (65). The second, that such courses would prevent the high degree of drop out — a dramatic trait in French universities which often rises as high as 60 per cent over a three year university course, though subject to differences depending on the particular faculty involved.

As far as the first claim is concerned, it would appear that the IUT's do attract a different social class of student. Table 7.2 sets out the social class origins of students at university and at the IUTs for two years — 1967 / 8 and 1973 / 4. This allows us to see how far the student body has changed from the early stages in the development of the IUTs and their present position. In addition, it also shows the distribution of the same social classes amongst the total French population in 1970 / 1 and in 1964 / 5.

Generally speaking the IUTs attract almost double the proportion of students from an agricultural or from a working class background compared to the university. But, as we see from the table, these two 'disadvantaged' social groups are still underrepresented in the 'new structure' when one compares them to the total population. Equally, children of industrialists, students with parents in liberal professions and from homes in the *cadres moyens* categories are still overrepresented, though in the case of the first two, by no means so much as in the university.

If one looks at this table from the standpoint of trends over time, it is interesting to note a slight increase in the proportion of children from agricultural and working class homes over the six year period. On the other hand, there seems equally to be a drive by the children of the 'liberal professions' into the IUTs as well.

Such developments are particularly interesting when placed in the broader perspective of the evolution in 'educational strategy' of the various social groups *vis a vis* higher education in France. A recent study by the *Secrétariat d'Etat aux Universités* shows clearly that children from working class or agricultural backgrounds have moved over the past decade towards the IUTs and to humanities faculties in particular (66). A similar tendency seems to be at work amongst the children of industrialists. There is what one might term a 'split strategy', some going for short course studies in the IUTs others opting for paramedical and scientific studies at university (67). Amongst the *cadres moyens* the general pattern that emerged over the decade was one in which no apparent strategy developed. Students from this background *s'orientent pour la plupart indifféremment dans toutes les disciplines de l'université* (68).

Certainly, as regards the social class of IUT students, these 'new structures' appear to be more 'democratic' than the traditional university. But this is only one indicator, and a parlous one at that. What do we know about the educational background of entrants to the IUTs?

In 1973, a special study was undertaken for the OECD on students in this new institution. With a sample drawn from eight IUTs — five in university towns and three in non-university agglomerations, the inquiry was based on 1824 students, of whom 60 per cent were in the first year and 40 per cent in the second. The sample population was stratified according to the economic sector — secondary or tertiary — for which their courses prepared them (69).

It is a particularly important inquiry since it allows us to determine to what extent the IUTs have managed to realize some of the hopes placed upon them early in their development. It is apparent, nonetheless, that little attempt has been made to admit students by the 'second route', by allowing *non bachelier* to sit a special examination. Ninety per cent of entrants were *bacheliers*. Only 4.1 per cent had taken the special examination (70). In other words, the IUTs are still restricted, in reality to the classic method of entry. Here it would seem the intentions of the legislation have not been met by members of the selection committees. This, however, does not mean to say that the IUT has totally failed to bring about changes in the educational background of students entering from school. Almost 60 per cent of the boys held a technician's baccalaureat, though approximately 50 per cent of the girls entered on the traditional baccalaureat A. Hitherto, the technician's baccalaureat constituted somewhat of an educational dead end.

Often it was taken by students who, earlier in their school careers, had been removed from tracks leading to the traditional baccalaureat. Though it leads to the *Brevet de Technicien Supérieur* it did not confer the right to enter university. The replacement of the *Brevet de Technicien* by the *Baccalaureat de Technicien* does, however, allow those holding it to enter certain university faculties, and as such constitutes an important contribution towards equalizing educational opportunity. It means, in effect, that able students are not penalized by dint of having made — or more likely, been forced to make — what higher education in times past was apt to regard as a 'wrong choice'.

Thus the educational background of students entering the IUTs places them in two distinct groups — those with the technician's baccalaureat and those with the 'classical' baccalaureat. However, there are other ways in which recruitment is differentiated as well. The former are apt to be more able — at least insofar as examination performance indicates ability — than the latter (71). Nor is it particularly surprising to find that students from the upper social classes were more likely to have attempted other studies in higher education before enrolling in the IUTs. One-third of upper class students were in this position. By contrast, if the IUTs were the last refuge for the scions of the middle classes, it was often the only institution to which students from less advantaged homes applied.

There are other ways in which one may suggest the IUTs are contributing to the equality of educational opportunity. Many of their students come from large families. Unfortunately, we do not have any comparable information which would allow us to assess this phenomenon against similar characteristics in the university student corpus. Nevertheless, this aspect should perhaps be emphasized for two reasons: first, because it is rarely used as an index variable to evaluate equality of educational opportunity at the higher levels of education systems; second, because it would appear to be an 'unexpected spin off', not intended by the legislator. Two-thirds of IUT students came from families of three or more children, and at least one in four were the youngest member of their family (72). Such a characteristic was independent of social class.

The degree to which the IUTs can effectively contribute to equalizing educational opportunity within the parameters set by legislation is, as we have pointed out, limited. There are possibilities for creating a 'non sequential' relationship with secondary education, but, like the issue of admissions qualifications, the initiative does not seem to have been grasped, either by applicants or by admissions committees. Hence, for the majority of students the relationship with secondary education is still 'sequential'. Ninety-five per cent of entrants are still less than 22 years of age (73). This suggests that, generally speaking, students enter the IUTs directly from school. The development of non sequential entry remains latent, and a future possibility.

There is certainly provision for development in this area. One of the most significant is the creation of the *Diplôme Universitaire de Technologie* (DUT) for adults which can be taken within the framework of the adult education programme (*promotion supérieure du Travail*). Obviously the existence of such a programme, as well as the special year for students already qualified and holding the first level DEUG, which allows them to pass the DUT in one year, rather than two, are important examples of areas where potential development might take place. But, on the basis of the empirical studies at our disposal, however promising as a future development, they have yet to be realized in any significant degree.

Originally, the IUTs were conceived as a short course, specialized institute within the legal framework of the university. They were not regarded as providing a jumping off point for further study. Indeed, had they been seen in this light, they would have conformed to a totally different model of institution, bearing more resemblance to the Yugoslavian or to the Norwegian 'multiple access model'. Yet, it would appear that this is a role towards which they are evolving, at least for certain groups of students. Hence, students' intentions and plans for future study are, effectively, changing the nature of the institution and thus acting as one of the 'covert' forces for institutional development which we mentioned earlier in this report. To a considerable degree the intention to embark upon 'long course' university studies after completion of the *Diplôme Universitaire de Technologie* is a function of social class. 51.3 per cent of students from an upper class background intended to continue study compared with 31.6 per cent of working class students (74). In short, the IUTs are developing, it would appear, into an 'indirect method' of gaining a place at university, a characteristic not dissimilar to recent developments in the UK with the colleges of further education. That 36 per cent of all IUT students wish to continue to long course studies has been seen as a fundamental conflict with the original objectives laid down by the government of these institutions (75). But one cannot deny, that by the same token, the IUTs are providing a route of access to higher education at one remove and thus contributing to equality of educational opportunity, even if that equality should in effect be outside the original legislative parameters.

B. *Norway: the district colleges*

The statistics relating to the regional colleges in Norway remain, as yet, extremely sparse. Hence, the information at our disposal does not allow us fully to evaluate the degree to which they are contributing to the equality of educational opportunity. Indeed, most of the published work is apt to stress, first, the experimental nature of these colleges; and second, the objectives and intentions ascribed to them, rather than undertaking an assessment of their performance to date. A recent account of these institutions points to a number of ways in which they might be fulfilling the task of equalizing educational opportunity, but in the main, it relies more on impressions than statistics. Students in the regional colleges tend to be somewhat older than university students at similar levels of study. Many of them have been at work between leaving school and entering the college (76). In part, this is due to a considerable number who attended vocational schools, rather than passing through the upper secondary school. Around 20 per cent in 1973 had come from seaman's schools, technical schools and similar institutions (77). Obviously, this situation suggests a far greater proportion of indirect entrants, than say, the IUTs in France. But it is extremely difficult to estimate to what extent the student body of this institution is composed of students coming in from work if one relies on official statistics alone.

One rule of thumb would be to take all those age 25 or over, on the grounds that, all students in this category would have to have spent some time in employment. On such a basis we see that the regional colleges are rapidly increasing both the proportion and especially the absolute numbers of indirect entrants. The results are reported in Table 7.3.

Table 7.3: Proportion of students aged 25 + in regional colleges by year

Year	1970	1971	1972	1973
% 25 +	12.1	20.6	21.9	20.0
N =	446	938	1677	2345

Source: NOS *Undervisningsstatistikk: Fag och Yrkesskoler* by year. Students enrolled on 1st October of stipulate year.

A second criterion that gives us some idea of the extent to which these establishments are moving towards an easier access to post-secondary education is to examine the number of students entering without *formal* matriculation qualifications. In this connexion, however, it is worthwhile recalling that entry to the regional colleges is selective. The number of applicants is two to three times the number of places (78). Table 7.4 sets out the proportion of students in regional colleges who entered without the formal matriculation examination.

Table 7.4: Proportion of students in regional colleges entering without formal matriculation qualifications

Year	1970	1971	1972	1973
Proportion 'unqualified'	4.3	16.0	18.2	17.1
N =	446	938	1677	2345

Source: NOS *Undervisningsstatistikk: Fag och Yrkesskoler, op. cit*

This, of course, does not provide any indication of the total number of unsuccessful unqualified applicants. But, even on this limited data we can suggest that the regional colleges appear, through their admission policy, to be more 'liberal' than the French IUTs, where only four per cent availed themselves of the entrance examination. (See *supra*, p. 81). And furthermore, they appear to have fulfilled one of their major objectives, namely to develop a non sequential relationship of higher to secondary education, though to what extent remains unclear at present.

C. *United Kingdom: the polytechnics*

The diversity of courses available in polytechnics poses particular methodological problems when comparing them to the universities. Furthermore, it also poses problems of evaluation. There are at least two levels on which one may conduct an evaluation of the development of these institutions: first, by comparing the characteristics of students on degree courses with their university fellows; second, by examining the relationship between degree and non-degree courses as it evolves inside the polytechnics.

Taking degree course students first, we find two outstanding differences between those in polytechnics and those in university; polytechnic students tend to come from a lower social class than their university counterparts: they also tend to be less well qualified, in the sense that they did not possess the formal A-levels required for university entrance. The results are reported in Table 7.5.

Table 7.5: Social class and educational background of degree level students in polytechnics compared with degree level students at university

Social class (% manual)		Percentage with 'other qualifications'	
University	Polytechnics	University	Polytechnics
27%*	36%**	2.1%	26%

Sources:
* UCCA *Statistical Supplement to the Eleventh Report*, Cheltenham, 1972.
** J. Whitburn, M. Mealing, C. Cox and S. Robinson, *Report on the Polytechnic Survey*, London, 1975, Polytechnic of North London (mimeo). Department of Education and Science. *Statistics of Education, Vol. 2. GCE, CSE and school-leavers*, 1972.

Since the survey on which these figures are based included some 9,000 students in 28 of the existing 30 polytechnics in 1971 / 2, it is a particularly reliable index of the extent to which the polytechnics seem to be implementing a policy of an *omnivalence des diplômes*.

Another indicator that is equally relevant to assessing how far the polytechnics are opening up higher education to social and educational groups hitherto excluded is to be found when one controls for the type of degree course. Prior to the development of the CNAA, degree courses undertaken by these establishments were usually an external degrees controlled by a neighbouring university. Effectively, this meant that conditions of entry were imposed from outside the institution. The transition to internally set, externally moderated degree courses presents a particularly important step in the development of the polytechnics. In addition, it may represent an opportunity by which the relatively strict requirements imposed by the university can be relaxed. If one takes as a minimum entrance requirement the possession of two A-levels, it is clear that CNAA degrees are more liberal in their demands compared with university external degree courses. Six per cent of polytechnic students following this level of course by the external system did not hold the minimum qualifications compared with 21 per cent of those enrolled for CNAA degrees (79). It would appear, therefore, that the CNAA courses are providing opportunities at undergraduate level for students not possessing the 'traditional' qualifications to enter higher education. To a large extent, however, polytechnic degree courses fulfil the role of 'mopping up' the excess demand for university level study which the universities themselves are unwilling to admit. This emerged with startling clarity when students were asked why they chose the polytechnics. Forty-four per cent of those enrolled for CNAA degrees did so because their A-level grades were inadequate to gain them a university place (80). So far the evidence we have presented suggests that polytechnics are affording some degree of equality first, by a more liberal policy as regards entrance conditions and second, by providing those places for students who would not otherwise have got into university. This approach is fully in what we have termed the 'logistical' interpretation of educational opportunity (see *supra* Chapter 1, pp. 14—15). In fine, it is the Robbins principle transferred from university to the non-university sector. But what evidence is there of a compensatory mechanism in the sense that mature students may also have similar opportunities of post-secondary education?

There are two ways in which we can examine this aspect of the problem; the first involves looking at the proportion of students aged 25 and over, the second, their level of qualification. Table 7.6 sets out the proportion of students aged 25 + according to the type of course in which they were enrolled.

Table 7.6: Proportion of students in various types of courses in polytechnics aged 25 +

Course	Degree	Other full-time *	Other part-time **	All polytechnic students
Percent	11	19	47	27
N =	4122	2003	2910	9035

Source: Withburn, Mealing *et al.*, *op. cit.*, p. 72, Table 43.

NB: *These categories are not the same as those normally used in the official statistics which distinguish between level — i.e. advanced and non-advanced — and study mode — i.e. sandwich, part-time day and part-time evening courses. In effect the group 'other full-time' includes students in sandwich courses, both of an advanced and non-advanced level, as well as full-time non-advanced students.
** Other part time includes both day and evening classes engaged in advanced and non-advanced levels of study.

From this we can see that the non sequential relationship of secondary and higher education is particularly developed in the case of students following part-time courses, where almost half are 'mature' students. This relationship is especially important for working class students, providing them, as it does with a second route over and above the normal full-time study pattern. This can be seen from Table 7.7 which sets out the social class background of students according to their various modes of study.

Table 7.7: Social background of students in various types of polytechnic course 1971 / 2

Working class *	Degree level	Other full-time	Other part-time	All polytech. students
per cent	36	35	49	40
N =	4122	2003	2910	9035

Source: Whitburn, Mealing *et al.*, *op. cit.*, p. 72.

It is at this point, however, that we turn to the evolution of the polytechnics over time. For despite the evidence that they are more open in their entrance conditions, and have managed to open themselves to a higher proportion of working class students following degree courses than the university, there is also some reason for arguing that this development has been at the expense of part-time and evening classes. The basis of this argument, put forward by Pratt and Burgess in a recent report on polytechnics, depends on a particular interpretation of their original purpose. 'One of the main implicit social objectives of the (polytechnic) policy, they argue, was the retention of a route for working and working class students.' (81). And, furthermore, that polytechnics should reflect a 'comprehensive community' of widely differing levels of course and patterns of study. Their evidence was drawn from a study of institutions which, designated as polytechnics in 1968 / 9, were then examined in the light of changes in the various methods of study available to their students from 1965 onwards. The analysis undertaken by Pratt and Burgess went no further than the year 1969 / 70. As more up to date information has since become available, we have extended this up to 1972 / 3, the latest point at which statistics have been published.

In Table 7.8 we show the distribution of the various types of course amongst designated institutions for the period 1965 to 1972, for advanced students only.

There are four features which stand out from this table. The first is the steady decline in the number of polytechnic students enrolled in external degrees at university, a development which reflects the growing autonomy of the polytechnics. The second is the expansion in the proportion of those students embarked upon CNAA degree courses. This is the reverse side of the same coin. The third is the very marked drop in the proportion of students engaged upon Higher National Certificate Courses from one in three in 1965 / 6 to just under one in ten by 1971 / 2. The fourth, which goes in the same direction is the fall off in the proportion of advanced polytechnic students enrolled in professional studies. This process, termed by Pratt and Burgess as one of 'academic drift', involves a decline in precisely those areas of study which attract working class students and mature students in particular.

Another way of presenting this highly complex table is to break it down into degrees and post-degree level courses and those of sub-degree level. This demands we collapse the first five rows up to and including postgraduate and research students to form the former category and the remainder to form the latter. (See Table 7.9.)

This suggests that the process detected by Pratt and Burgess in the early stages of polytechnic development has, in effect, continued, as the 'new structures' tend, increasingly to assume a priority of study very similar to the university. Thus, against the undoubted expansion in educational opportunity compared to the universities, one has to set a process of 'institutional reproduction' by which the polytechnics

Table 7.8: Distribution of students in various courses in polytechnics from 1965 to 1972 (advanced students only) (%).

Year	First univ.	Degree CNAA	Higher univ.	Degree CNAA	PG+research	HND	HNC	Art	Professional studies	Other	Total N=
1965/6	14.0	4.9	0.7	—	2.6	6.0	29.1	4.4	30.5	6.5	76.920*
1966/7	13.0	6.9	0.4	0.04	3.4	6.9	23.5	5.3	34.0	8.3	95.066*
1967/8	12.6	9.4	0.6	0.07	3.5	7.6	21.2	5.0	32.7	7.4	100.813*
1968/9	11.2	13.0	0.6	0.13	4.2	8.6	14.8	3.6	31.2	12.6	101.994*
1969/70	9.7	20.0	0.3	0.32	4.8	10.6	12.4	3.8	28.7	9.4	91.080*
1970/1	9.6	22.1	0.5	0.42	4.4	10.1	11.7	3.8	27.5	9.9	111.283
1971/2	7.9	26.0	0.40	0.65	4.6	9.4	10.9	4.0	26.3	9.8	114.147

Sources: Pratt and Burgess, *The Polytechnics a Report, op. cit.,* p. 76.
* DES *Statistics of Education, vol. 3, Further Education,* HMSO, by year.

Note: Table to be read across the rows which sum to 100.

Table 7.9: Proportion of degree to non-degree students in polytechnics 1965 / 6 to 1971 / 2 — advanced students only

Year	Degree or post-degree study Per cent	Sub-degree study Per cent	N = *
1965 / 6	22	78	76.920
1968 / 9	29	71	101.994
1969 / 70	35	65	91.080
1970 / 1	37	63	111.283
1971 / 2	40	60	114.147

Source: same as above.

appear to be moving towards a model in which degree level courses predominate. A parallel development appears also to be taking place in respect of the proportion of full-time to part-time students. The extent to which polytechnics are acquiring 'academic status' by throwing overboard their part-timers can be gathered from Table 7.10, which shows the position with respect of all enrolments in this type of institution, rather than concentrating on advanced students only as have the two previous tables.

Table 7.10: Ratio of full time to part-time students (total enrolments) in polytechnics on November 1st of each year

November 1st	Full-time Per cent	Part-time Per cent	Total enrolment N =
1965*	27	73	169.741
1966*	30	70	175.580
1967*	34	66	171.698
1969	42	58	41.076
1970	41	59	144.068
1971	46	54	162.852
1972	49	51	159.292
1973**	50	50	153.319

Sources: * Pratt and Burgess, *op. cit.*, p. 72, Table X. DES, *Statistics of Education, vol. 3, Further Education*, HMSO, by year.
** Report from the Committee of Polytechnic Directors quoted in *Times Higher Educational Supplement*, March 15, 1974, p. 18.

When we consider that the proportion of working class students and also mature students is highest in the part-time areas of study, the shift in emphasis between full-time and part-time courses in these institutions seems to uphold the interpretation advanced by Pratt and Burgess. And whilst there is reason to hope that, from a qualitative standpoint, the polytechnics are admitting socially and educationally deprived and underrepresented groups, from the quantitative point of view, the same institution seems bent upon doing precisely the opposite.

This development, perhaps more than any other, reinforces two propositions. First, that the creation of 'new structures' may, in the first instance, help towards the equality of educational opportunity at the outset. But this does not mean they will continue so to do. Structures, however defined, are prey to their internal tensions which can often divert them from their 'objective'. This we saw in the case of the French IUTs as well. The second point serves merely to emphasize the first. Studies based on a single point in time do not allow us to estimate the way in which institutional factors impinge upon such matters as equality of educational opportunity. *Satisfaction and self congratulation in one year, does not mean one can continue in a spirit of self admiration the next. Rather what is required is a continual monitoring process so that public policy may intervene to encourage those institutions remaining on the path of their objectives and act to restore those who, by chance and unintentionally, have 'gone off course'.*

D. *United Kingdom: the Open University*

So far we have examined the extent to which various educational institutions contribute towards equality of educational opportunity from the point of view of access conditions, and the characteristics of students entering them compared with the 'conventional' university. Yet, educational opportunity has little meaning if the easier the terms of access the greater the drop-out rate. Effectively, such a development merely endorses the equal right of students to fail. Whether or not such consequences can be said to provide equality or the type of equality envisaged by legislators, governments and educationists is a different matter. Certainly, the problem is a particularly acute one.

It is in this particular context, that the Open University is especially important. The significance of this institution is two fold: first, it represents the possibility of open access to all levels of the population and therefore is the first stage by which the pejorative connotations of 'dropping out' can give way before the idea of 'stopping out' to 'drop in' later; second, because it represents an attempt to create an establishment based on the individual-centred interpretation of

educational opportunity within a system which, in varying degrees
contains the two other ideologies as well. In short, it is the final
representative of a 'pluralistic' system of higher education rather than
the monolithic structure dictated by the university. This is all the more
important when we consider that, in the light of our evidence on
polytechnics, institutional reproduction seems, quantitatively at least to
be curtailing educational opportunity at the sub-degree level.

. The Open University is, then an important venture, as much from
the standpoint of its structural innovation as from the light its setting
up might cast upon the general problems associated with introducing
greater equality of opportunity in higher education. This being so, at
the risk of unbalancing the amount of attention devoted to this
institution, we will pursue a more detailed analysis than we have
hitherto with the others.

Data on the educational background of students applying to and
finally enrolling in, the Open University is far more copious and
comprehensive than that available for polytechnics which tend to
concentrate on administrative and curricular developments rather than
on detailed student follow up studies. Table 7.11 shows the proportion
of provisionally registered students not having the 'minimum university
entrance requirements' of two or more A-levels and the type of
qualification they do hold, for the years 1971 to 1975.

This table shows without peradventure the compensatory role
fulfilled by the Open University insofar as it permits the entry of
totally unqualified applicants. In 1975, for example, one student in ten
of all provisionally registered possessed no public certificates
whatsoever. Given the way in which the polytechnics survey was
conducted, it is not possible to compare directly the qualifications held
by students with 'other qualifications' with their Open University
counterparts. But even if we assume the likelihood that some of the
polytechnic degree course students hold similar qualifications to some
of the 'non-qualified' in the Open University study, it is nevertheless
evident that the formal 'ability range' as measured by the possession or
the absence of examination certificates is wider in the Open University
than in polytechnics. Indeed, even if we were able to compare the
educational background of degree level students at polytechnics with
those in the Open University, the differences that would emerge would
in all probability, be an underestimate on the side of the OU. This is
because many of the OU students will have used part of the inter-
vening period between school and entry to a degree level course to
gain additional educational qualifications in the further education
sector.

A more recent study carried out in relation to the 1971 entry of
students to the Open University is especially important here. An

Table 7.11: **Educational background of provisionally registered students by year of registration**

Educational qualifications	1971 %	1972 %	1973 %	1974 %	1975 %
None	6.8	8.6	9.1	8.5	11.2
CSE / RSA	1.8	3.8	3.8	2.9	3.6
1–4 O-levels	5.9	7.6	8.1	8.0	10.2
5+ O-levels	10.8	12.8	12.3	10.8	12.9
1 A-level	3.5	4.2	4.1	4.3	4.7
Total 'non-qualified'	28.8	37.0	37.4	34.5	42.6
Total 'qualified'	71.2	63.0	62.6	65.5	57.4
N=	24.220	20.501	16.895	14.976	19.823

Source: Naomi McIntosh and Alan Woodley 'Excellence, equality and the Open University', paper delivered to the *3rd International Conference on Higher Education, Lancaster*, 1975, p. 7 (xerox).

Table 7.12: **Reasons given for not applying to the Open University by occupation and terminal age of education, 1975 cohort**

Reasons for not applying	Occupation			Terminal Age of Education	
	House-wives	Education	Manual workers	15–	21+
No courses in subject of interest	15	15	22	18	19
Inability to specialize	11	14	12	11	15
Possible non-recognition of degree	3	5	8	4	7
Unable to attend summer school	46	12	31	39	17
Financial commit-ment too great	36	14	25	31	16
Courses too difficult	9	1	10	14	1
Type of job makes OU study difficult	2	5	26	16	7
Would not help job prospects	3	3	8	7	6
Care of children	52	9	4	15	13
Not enough time for studying	28	31	30	29	29

Source: McIntosh and Woodley, *Excellence and equality, op. cit.*, p. 11 Table 6.

examination of the type of school which OU students had spent the greatest number of years showed that over half (58 per cent) of all students had attended academic selective schools (grammar schools). Even amongst manual workers the proportion going to grammar school was as high as 46 per cent (82). 'Only a minority' the report noted, 'about one-third genuinely appear to have been disadvantaged at the *initial* level, i.e. not having been given the opportunity to study at a grammar or an equivalent level school.' (83). This would seem to point to a well-known phenomenon in education namely, the extent to which the individual wishes to gain more education at a post-school level depends highly on his secondary school experience. Or in more biblical terms 'to him who already hath had, it shall be given'. Another, and equally potent factor in deciding initial applications to the Open University is, of course, the present work situation in which the individual finds him or herself. An investigation into the factors prompting students *not* to apply to the university, after an initial inquiry, revealed five main dimensions of 'deterrance'. These were, problems associated with attendance at the compulsory summer schools arranged for OU students, cost, work load and course provision as well as the perception of the relevance of courses. 'These' the investigation suggested, 'will continue to make the University less "open" for women, for blue collar workers, for the old and for those who completed their full-time education at an early age.' (84).

Hence, realization of educational opportunity is dependent on factors that were noted by another study undertaken by the *Institut d'Education* in connexion with educational leave policies in various European countries — namely, the individual's present position in the occupational structure (85).

The main question this raises in turn is 'What are the perceived barriers to enrolment in the Open University?'. How do they differ between the various social classes? What do they tell us about the problems associated with the realization of equality of opportunity in education? Table 7.12 sets out some of the reasons for not applying to the Open University for selected occupational groups and also by the student's terminal age of education (TEA).

If we take for each of the three occupational groups, the three most frequently endorsed difficulties we find first, that housewives are constrained by care of children, by inability to attend summer school and by the expense involved in enrolment. For those in occupations associated with education the major obstacle occurs with not having enough time for study, lack of interesting courses and, in equal third position, the inability to specialize in their study and the financial cost. For manual workers, the main difficulties are the inability to attend summer school, lack of time for study and obstacles created by the type of job they are engaged in.

What this table reveals, in a very succint manner, is that once an institution, dedicated to the individual centred ideology of educational opportunity, throws down the structural and qualificatory barriers associated with entry to higher education, it merely reveals the fundamental social-structural barriers that lurk beneath the more ostensible pedagogic hurdles. And, in so doing, not only poses new questions about the anatomy of educational opportunity, but also shows how crude were the assumptions on which previous definitions rested in the past.

So far, we have examined the educational background and some of the reasons for non-application. But an important element in educational opportunity is contained in the flow patterns of students through the institution. By tracing students through various stages from entry to graduation we can see at which point certain groups fall by the wayside. For both men and women, those in manual, clerical and office jobs, in sales and service work as well as those not working were less likely to accept an offer of a place. Effectively, as an OU report recently observed, the main problem in creating equal opportunities for underrepresented groups in higher education to have easier access to it, lies in the pre-application period. 'At every stage from actually hearing of the OU to accepting the offer of a place, barriers exist which discriminate against particular types of people, many of whom have been deprived of educational opportunities in the past' (86).

The structure of the Open University's enrolment process involves students registering provisionally for a foundation course in the first year. This is a trial period of three months. If they continue, they pay the final registration fee and thus acquire the status of an OU student, able to leave or to rejoin as they wish. Around 75 per cent of provisionally registered students decide to enrol definitely and of these 80 per cent succeed in their first year studies. Table 7.13 shows the proportion of finally registered students of a particular year still studying in subsequent years.

But this general picture hides certain significant differences in the flow pattern of students holding A-levels or their equivalent and the 'unqualified'. Slightly fewer 'unqualified' students finally registered, compared to the 'qualified', and moreover, those who did register were less likely to gain a credit, the most marked differences being found in mathematics and those following social science courses (87). And, finally, manual workers were less likely to obtain a credit in the course they enrolled in. Taking the students gaining a credit as a proportion of all those who finally registered, 75.6 per cent of non-manual students gained a credit compared to 54.9 per cent for those in manual occupations (88).

Table 7.13: **Proportion of students registered in a particular year still studying in subsequent years**

		Year registered		
per cent		1971	1972	1973
re-enrolled	N =	19.581	15.716	12.680
in following				
years		%	%	%
	1971	100		
	1972	83	100	
	1973	68	79	100
	1974	54	67	81
	1975	41	53	69

Source: McIntosh and Woodley, *op. cit.*, p. 21.

Viewed from the standpoint of evolution over time, it would appear that this pattern between the performance of 'qualified' compared with 'non-qualified' students and the achievement of 'non-manual' compared to manual students is becoming more sharply accentuated. An examination of the differences in achievement between the four groups over the four years from 1971 to 1975 suggests that, though the Open University is managing to attract relatively more students in working class occupations and those with lower educational qualifications, they are performing less well during their first year. In fine, the more open to all social groups the OU becomes, the greater the attrition rate at the end of the first year, a phenomenon not dissimilar to the 'open door' policy instituted for mature students in the Swedish university.

There remains one final question: How does the OU's student body compare with the classic university with respect of its social class composition? The normal method of ascertaining this for university statistics is to take the occupation of the parents. Since OU students are not economically dependent on their family, we will show both the individual's occupational status and that of his parents. Despite the enormous expansion in the numbers entering the traditional university in the post-war period, the social class of the student body has, proportionately, remained virtually static. In 1929, for example 27 per cent of university students came from working class homes. Forty-two years later in 1971 this had risen to 29 per cent, though even this slight change is somewhat suspect since it occured at a time when the Universities Central Council on Admissions altered its sampling method (89).

Table 7.14: Occupational status of OU students, of their fathers and of economically active males in Great Britain, aged 45—59

	OU students		Fathers' status	Univ. Students	1966 Census
	1971	1973	1972		
Administrators and managers	6	5	7	14	6
Scientists, liberal prof. education	76	69	14	30	8
Routine non manual	14	18	28	27	22
Manual	5	8	52	29	64

Source: Naomi McIntosh, and Judith A. Calder, *A Degree of Difference, op. cit.*, p. 138, Table 2.

If we use the normal criteria of judging the occupational background of students — that is their father's occupation — we find that the Open University comprises over half its students from working class homes and an additional 28 per cent in routine non-manual occupations. This is certainly a dramatic improvement on the situation in 'classical' universities. And, if one compares the distribution of students from working class homes at the OU with the census figures for 1966, this hitherto highly underrepresented group comes much nearer the national occupational distribution for the relevant age group. In fine, the Open University is attracting large numbers of students from those groups in society which are occupationally mobile. An examination of the present occupational status of student intakes between 1971 and 1973 does, however, reveal an increase in the proportion of students in working class occupations from five to eight per cent over the two years. Similarly, there is also an increase in the number of students in routine white collar occupations as well.

In summary the Open University is contributing to the equality of educational opportunity in two ways: by providing a second route for adults to pursue degree level courses who, for one reason or another, did not continue to higher education; and by providing an opportunity for those without the formal qualifications to enter university. If the first role can be identified with an almost Robbins-like interpretation of the availability of talent, the second extends this principle. The availability of talent is not identified by various institutional criteria so much as by individual motivation, aspiration and self betterment. But in moving from the liberal to the 'radical' interpretation of educational opportunity, the OU reveals some of the grosser structural obstacles attendant upon various occupational situations. The majority of students in the Open University are upwardly mobile, a mobility secured by previous qualifications in or after leaving school. To this extent, it would seem that it has still to penetrate to those groups in society — working class in the main — for whom compensatory strategies are most relevant, but hardest to realize. 'In some respects', a recent article commented, 'the Open University seems still to be falling short of its original goals' (90).

Essentially, the Open University has revealed a fundamental conflict contained in the notion of 'compensatory' education. It is important to explain this conflict since 'compensatory education' lies at the heart of the radical interpretation of equality in educational opportunity. On the one side, is the belief that compensatory strategies should help to remove those traditional obstacles to higher education that prevent the emergence of 'active demand' for extended education amongst deprived groups. This, the Open University seems well on the way to meeting. On the other side, is the notion that, contained in a more radical view of 'compensative education', is the duty to stimulate those groups in society to demand higher education which previously would not have done so. In short, of actively encouraging what has hitherto remained a 'passive demand' or a total unwillingness of certain groups to continue education at all. Whilst the first policy seems to benefit the socially mobile, the second demands what one can only term a policy of 'social mobilization' to overcome those factors — such as public environment — which produce low levels of attainment amongst certain social groups. *Without this second strategy, the benefits that result from open access could well be even more dependent upon attainment and attitudes towards education in general, attitudes engendered in the secondary school, in the home, and on the shopfloor.*

E. *Yugoslavia: the vise skole*

In contrast to the development of the other 'new structures' in higher education, the quantitative role of the *vise skole* in the Yugoslavian system has declined. Up to 1967 / 8, the proportion of its total enrolments continued to expand, reaching 39 per cent of all students in higher education. From then on, student flows appear to have altered directing themselves into the university. Hence, by 1973 / 4, only 29 per cent of the total enrolments in Yugoslavian higher education were in the *vise skole*. Table 7.15 sets out the proportion of students enrolled in this institution from 1965 / 6 to 1973 / 4.

As originally conceived, the *vise skole* stood in sharp contrast to the binary model of higher education found in the polytechnics, and the specialized model found in the shape of the IUTs. It represented — at least in its earlier phase of development — what has been termed the multiple access model of post-secondary education. More recently, particularly in the early part of the 1970s it has reverted to what might be called a semi-specialized institution, with features similar to both the IUTs and also the English polytechnics. Effectively, the imposition of somewhat rigid conditions for transfer from the *vise skole* to university have served, in part at least, to deviate this institution from its original intention.

The main aims of the *vise skole* were, as we have seen previously two fold: first, to provide new technical personnel required by an evolving economy; second, to develop a basic two year education leading either directly into the labour market or on to further study at university. In addition, a further objective was to give the opportunity for adults already engaged in work, the opportunity of having access to higher education. One of the major problems of such short course institutions is the type of jobs to which their courses lead. Since, the explicit aim of the *vise skole* is to provide industry, commerce and administration with intermediary cadres and personnel, there is the distinct risk that such a function rebounds upon the prestige of the particular institution. This may have a number of consequences. First, that what appears to be the democratization of higher education through the greater participation of groups hitherto excluded from higher education is, in effect, but a disguised form of differentiation. Second, that whilst the intention is to provide both short and ultimately access to long cycle courses, in reality the institution becomes identified with short cycle education, and thus reverts to a position not dissimilar to the binary policy of comparatively rigid separation between the two sectors. In short, the relationship thus created produces in higher education the well known phenomenon of 'parity of esteem' in secondary education between 'academic' institutions on the one hand, and technical / vocational bodies on the other. The principal issue posed by such multiple access types of institution is: how far are manpower planning requirements compatible with the other explicit goal of equalizing educational opportunity?

One of the main considerations prompting the creation of the *vise skole* was the belief that short cycle, vocationally-oriented education would prove more attractive to students from working class homes as well as to those currently employed. This would appear to be so. Table 7.16 sets out the proportion of students from various social classes enrolled for full time study at the various institutes of the Yugoslavian system of higher education.

The *vise skole* are particularly attractive to students from working class and agricultural backgrounds, whilst the university appears to draw

Table 7.16: Proportion of students by social class enrolled in various types of higher education institute (full time)

	N=	Univer-sities %	*Vise Skole %	Colleges %	Art academies %
Upper manage-ment	32.041	83	13.1	1.8	2.1
Army, police	11.404	82	15.5	1.4	1.1
Employees	22.258	78.5	17.6	2.8	1.2
Other prof. + non-active	12.200	75.9	20.7	0.6	1.9
Trading	5.264	75.1	21.8	2.4	0.7
Public services personnel	1.644	69.8	27.3	1.4	1.4
Workers	21.018	69.4	26.8	3.0	0.8
Transport personnel	4.279	67.8	29.0	2.7	0.5
Farmers	18.686	63.5	34.5	1.7	0.3
Non-response	2.738	76.7	20.7	0.6	1.9

Source: Philippe Cibois and Janina Markiewicz Lagneau, *Bilan de l'Enseignement Supérieur Court*, Paris, 1974, OCDE, p. 13, Table 1.2.

upon students from upper management and from families in the police or army. Certainly, on those criteria of manpower requirements, the *vise skole* are fulfilling their original intentions. A major expansion has taken place in departments of technical studies and applied sciences, areas particularly in demand (91). Moreover, the task of assuring part-time education for adults has virtually become the distinguishing mark of this type of institution, with much of the work being transferred from the university. Table 7.17 reveals this development most succinctly.

Table 7.17: Proportion of part time to full time students by type of institution and year

	Universities %	Vise Skole %
1961 / 2	27.4	56.3
1963 / 4	23.0	53.5
1965 / 6	21.0	54.1
1967 / 8	17.8	52.2
1969 / 70	17.1	50.3

Source: D. Furth (ed) *Short Cycle Higher Education, op. cit.*, p. 166.

Similar to the polytechnics in the sense of providing a second chance education through part-time study, the *vise skole* do not appear to have suffered from the academic drift observable in the British institutions, a drift characterized, as we noted earlier, by a shedding of large numbers of part-time students. The importance of this part-time function is readily graspable when one considers the age distribution of students in full and part-time study in the *vise skole*. A recent investigation undertaken in 1974, based on a sample of students enrolled in these institutions in the Croatian Republic, showed that whilst five per cent of full-time students were 25 years or older, 53.0 per cent of those on part-time study fell into this age range (92). Effectively, the role of second chance education seems assured, though not the role of 'compensatory education' in the sense noted in the Open University. This for the simple reason that the entry conditions to the *vise skole* do not permit the admission of other than formally qualified students.

The degree of differentiation between the *vise skole* and the university emerges with particular clarity when one examines the educational background and qualifications of its students. The majority — two-thirds — come from technical schools with the remainder from gymnasia or academic high schools. Furthermore there is a considerable difference in the educational attainment between the sexes. Girls entering for full-time study are likely to be highly qualified whereas boys tend to have mediocre levels of performance in the school leaving certificate (93). Far more important, however, is the fact that nine full-time students out of ten enrolled in this type of institution applied only to the *vise skole*. Only nine per cent applied to university (96). This suggests a high degree of structural differentiation between the two institutions, a differentiation exacerbated when one considers that the basic two year course has not been taken up with any alacrity by the universities. For this reason, comparison between the two institutions is difficult since the levels of study vary between the two.

Nevertheless, the *vise skole* do appear to be contributing to educational opportunity though in a manner which differs depending on the social class of individual students. For those from a relatively modest background, the *vise skole* enables them to take the first step in the higher education ladder, thus providing them both with a professional training they can use in the labour market, and with the possibility of converting to longer courses later. For students from the upper classes, the *vise skole* acts as a safety net, palliating their often poor performance in secondary school, and also, as a second route of entry to long course education once the initial two year period has been completed (95). For the former, the *vise skole* offers an opportunity to adjust to higher education through teaching methods not too dissimilar to those used in secondary education. For the latter, the *vise skole* acts to prevent dropping out and high wastage rates (96).

Though in theory, the two year post-secondary colleges provide a bridge between school and long course higher education, in reality, this opening appears to be of interest only to the younger entrants and amongst this group, young men from upper class background (97). In effect, though four students out of ten on full-time courses would like to continue their studies either full-time or on a part-time basis at the end of their time in the *vise skole*, there is a clear differentiation of functions depending on the age of the individual. The younger he or she is, the greater the intention of using the bridge into university study. For older students, however, the *vise skole* serves as a 'recycling' function, updating skills and allowing them to move higher up in the occupational hierarchy (98).

Within the limits set by the general objectives attributed to these colleges, objectives which were, in the main, inspired by manpower planning requirements, the *vise skole*, appears to have responded well. However, it is apparent that they are not completely masters in their own house. They are just as affected by changes in other sectors of the higher education system as they are by official legislative intention. For example, the fact that the universities are no longer prepared to recognize the validity of the two year course for transfer to university studies, unless the course contains certain elements regarded as a necessary prerequisite, has considerably altered the relationship between the two sectors. What this illustrates is, in fact, a fundamental feature of education systems undergoing transformation, namely, the enormous powers of inertia still to be found in the hierarchically and also historically 'superior' institutes in the educational pyramid.

The absence of particular information on the patterns of student flow to long course higher education via the *vise skole*, is of course, a major drawback. For without information in this domain there is little evidence to permit an assessment of the effectiveness of the 'second route', although it has been claimed that the *vise skole* have practically no opening into the university (99). Indeed, it is suggested that one of the main reasons why these colleges can fulfil their economic aims so well is precisely because of their hierarchical subordination to the university. Essentially, the function performed by the *vise skole* is directly in keeping with one of the principal aims enunciated early on in the debate over the future of the British polytechnics – that of 'matching' the education system's output to the changing needs of society (100). Perhaps, from this standpoint, there is a fundamental contradiction between meeting social demand for education by providing access to a university type course and, on the other, the need to meet economic demands which seem best served by creating institutions with separate goals, education, curriculum and ultimately clientele. *It is unlikely that the effects of social inequality will be eradicated simply by transposing the differences between long and short course education from the secondary to the post-secondary sectors.*

Discussion

As a summary we will attempt to give some indication of the extent to which the new structures have contributed towards creating the conditions necessary for equality in educational opportunity. We have seen in the course of this chapter that different countries have employed varying strategies in their attempts to create new methods of access to higher education. Some, like the IUTs, the *vise skole* and the Norwegian regional colleges have opted for a short course, professionally-oriented curriculum. Others, for example, the Open University and the polytechnics have opted for a more flexible pattern of 'long courses' in parallel to the traditional university mode of study. Some have broken with the pattern of 'sequential' education following on directly from secondary school. The *vise skole*, the Open University, the polytechnics, though the latter to a decreasing degree, have evolved part-time study for adults, a highly important contribution towards affording a second chance to those who, for one reason or for another, missed out on higher education when young. In an earlier chapter we suggested that the break down in the 'sequential' relationship between secondary and higher education was an important manifestation of the transition in the interpretation of educational opportunity from the socially oriented to the individual centred ideology (101). A final dimension in assessing the extent to which the various institutions have opened up higher education, is contained in the proportion of students aged 25 years or over.

This latter variable is somewhat arbitrary. But in the absence of any consistent information on whether entrants to the various 'new structures' came directly from school or from further education, it is reasonable to assume that those aged 25 and above are indirect entrants having spent a considerable time in employment. Their number therefore represents a crude indicator, *faute de mieux*, of the extent to which each type of institution has embarked upon a policy of 'educational recycling'. One can, of course, argue that this latter variable measures the same thing as the proportion of part-timers in a particular institute — to wit, the degree of 'sequentiality' or 'non sequentiality' between higher and secondary education. Whilst admitting this to be so, it does not necessarily follow that all who are part-time students are necessarily indirect entrants from the world of work. Some of them can just as well be direct entrants from school and should, in effect, be classified as part-time workers.

On the basis of these three variables — the proportion of students in part-time study, those aged 25 years or over, and the proportion of those admitted without the formally recognized qualifications necessary to enter a particular course, we can construct an 'educational opportunity index' to compare the various new structures one to another.

Table 7.18: Educational opportunity index for the new structures

Institution	Proportion of all enrolled who were Part-timers	Aged 25+	Not formally 'qualified'	Index*
IUTs	0%	1.3*[1]	6.1**[2]	7.4
Regional colleges	0%	12.1	16.0	28.1
Polytech.[3]	30.2	11.0	12.4	53.6
Open Univ.[4]	100.0	91.0	28.8	273.4
Vise Skole	50.3	23.4[5]	0	73.7

NB / *   The educational opportunity index is calculated by summing all figures greater than 0 in columns 1 thru 3.
1   Estimates.
2   Assumes that all who did not pass the Baccalaureat were admitted on examination and jury assessment.
3   Degree course students only. 1972 / 3.
4   1971 registered entrants.
5   On basis of sample survey for Croatia see Cibois and Markiewicz Lagneau, *op. cit.*

On the basis of these three criteria, it appears that the IUTs have made least contribution towards opening up post-secondary education. Their relationship is still sequential given that few students are aged 25 and over, and little attempt has been made to admit students on criteria other than those set by national public examination. At the other extreme, we have the Open University, where all students are engaged in part-time study, nine out of ten are aged 25 and over on admission and just over one in three do not have the requisite requirements that a degree level course would demand.

At this juncture, it is relevant to point out that the criterion variables are those which would be used for assessing the degree of opportunity within an individual centred framework of the term. And thus what we are assessing is the degree to which the new structures have moved towards non sequentiality in the relationship between secondary and higher education as well as the extent to which new structures have thus endorsed an individual centred interpretation of educational opportunity. But not all governments would endorse this and would, in consequence put forward other species of social indicators more in keeping with their particular aims or goals. It is conceivable, for example, that some might view part-time education as contributing little towards equality of educational opportunity on the grounds that it merely risks a greater drop out rate. If this is the case, then it would be reasonable to introduce such considerations as 'through put' in the various institutions we have examined. By 'through put' we mean the proportion of those qualifying at the end of the course who entered x years previously.

For others, the main criterion would be one of manpower planning needs. Hence, they would insist on examining the type of qualifications obtained by students at the end of their course to see how far this corresponded with perceived economic needs.

Obviously, the choice of variables depends to a very considerable extent on the particular priorities assigned to the various institutions, not all of which were, as we have pointed out, to equalize educational opportunity.

Part Three

Summary and Recommendations

Chapter 8

Towards the Attainment of Equality: Some Concluding Considerations

In this report we have examined the ways in which various institutes representing significant structural innovation in higher education have contributed towards equalizing educational opportunity. Briefly, there were three main approaches to this problem from the institutional standpoint. First, the traditional demand—response strategy, that is providing more places and accepting as valid for higher education diplomas which would not, in ordinary circumstances have gained their holder ready admission to university. Such a policy we see in train with the IUTs, the *Gesamthochschule* Kassel. The second, consisted in providing modes of study more suited to adults or those in part-time employment, though still demanding the possession of a formal qualification. Such is the position in the case of the *vise skole*, the district colleges in Norway and the polytechnics. A third strategy consisted in widening the 'student constituency' by more flexible entry conditions, by accepting those with diplomas not recognized as being equivalent to the school leaving certificate or even those without any formal qualification at all. Such a policy reached its most developed stage in the Open University, though to a lesser extent, the polytechnics appeared to operate one not too dissimilar. In Chapter 7, we constructed an index of educational opportunity, an index based upon three criteria — the proportion of the student body in these institutions studying part-time, the proportion aged 25 years and over, and the proportion admitted without formal qualifications. These variables, as we pointed out corresponded to an education system that was open in the sense of admitting 'second chance' students; open in that it did not depend totally upon what we have termed a 'sequential relationship' between secondary and higher education; open too in that access to higher education no longer depends on prior achievement in the secondary sector. *On the basis of this index, it would seem that the 'Open University' model has, much to offer those whose priorities in policy planning tend mainly to equalizing educational opportunity.*

It is at this point relevant perhaps to provide a brief summary of the extent to which the various institutions included in the investigation have — or have not — responded to the expectations placed upon them. We saw that the IUTs appear to attract students from relatively unfavoured backgrounds and that, compared to the university, the social class composition of their student body is far nearer the national occupational structure. However, it is highly unlikely that their modest contribution towards equalizing educational opportunity will have much impact upon the higher education system. Their expansion is not rapid enough — indeed it is falling behind the targets set. In addition to their apparent lack of attraction for certain types of student, it is nevertheless evident that the IUTs are subject to highly distortive forces. Thus, their institutional development has fallen far short of the legislative intention particularly with respect to the use to which they are put by their students — that is, as a stepping stone to higher education, rather than as an institution to training relevant to the world of work.

The *Gesamthochschule* Kassel remains as yet, in the experimental stage. None of its students have graduated, nor is there any statistical information that would allow one to assess its progress so far. Since its major purpose is devoted to curricular development, it would be extremely difficult to assess to what extent its curricular experiments had — or alternatively had not — succeeded. Such a study as this, relying on information about access conditions, social class and educational background of students would not reveal effectively the impact of such an institution within the limits of its own and publicly endorsed criteria. This would require an analysis on lines not dissimilar to the taxonomic studies of Benjamin Blum and his team and hence demand an evaluation of the degree to which students reached the formally defined objectives contained in the curriculum. Such an investigation is beyond both our remit and the time at our disposal.

The Norwegian district colleges appear to have fulfilled their defined aims, though access is paradoxically more difficult than it is to the universities.

The polytechnics, like the IUTs to a certain degree, appear to be engaged in that fatal chase after 'academic respectability'. Whilst their degree level students are drawn from a wider social and educational background, it is very evident that their expansion at the degree level has been at the expense of the sub-degree level students. As such this process is a particularly good illustration of the conflict between various definitions of educational opportunity. For on the one hand, the polytechnics have undoubtedly contributed much by comparison with the universities. On the other, they appear to reinforce the basic principle in education systems generally, namely 'to him that hath it shall be given. And to him who hath not, it shall be taken away even that which he hath' (Gospel according to St. Matthew). It is arguable that this shedding of part-time and sub-degree students does not entail any diminution of educational opportunity since an agreement has been reached by which colleges of further education take over the task of assuring the education of the sub-degree level students. What this seems to forget, however, is that the emergence of Institutes of Higher Education to cope with the supposedly new clientele sets at nought the original purpose, or at least that enunciated by the major spokesmen of the polytechnic lobby, namely that polytechnics were intended to cater for a more diverse student body by concentrating on the non-degree level students. Furthermore, the emergence of the Institutes of Higher Education would appear suspiciously like the resurrection at the higher education level of precisely that tripartite division between academic, technical and vocational education which is rapidly vanishing at the secondary level. This most recent development suggests that institutional reproduction is not the only danger present when the structures of higher education are changed to cope with a more broadly based clientele. *Institutional reproduction* is to a large extent, outside the control of administrative authorities and stems, in the main, from the desire of teaching personnel to enhance their standing by increased concentration on degree level courses. But *systems reproduction* — that is the recreation of structures that, hitherto abounded in one sector and their introduction into another — is surely within the control of governments. If it is not, then one must question the competence of the Ministry concerned.

From an historical standpoint, it would seem that there is one constant feature attached to educational policy formulation in the UK context, a feature as strong today as it was with the foundation of state education a century or more ago. That is, whenever mass education is introduced at various levels of education, primary in 1870, secondary in 1902 and 1944, higher in the 1970s, it is inevitably accompanied by a tripartite division of institutions. The history of educational development from a structural standpoint within the UK context is not one of *innovation*, but one of *substitution* involving the progressive relocation of a tripartite institutional pattern further up the education system.

The Open University, however, stands outside this particular tradition. But whilst one must recognize the fundamental contribution it is making towards equality of educational opportunity, one must also, by the same token, recognize that those who avail themselves of the facilities offered are, in the main, those who have already benefitted in large part from the secondary education system. The casting down of qualificatory barriers for admission to higher education seems to be of benefit mainly to those in middle class occupations. Yet, from another point of view, one of the most significant 'spins off' achieved by the Open University is to point to some of the less obvious elements and factors which act as obstacles to the achievement of equality of opportunity, even when this is envisaged in terms of the individual centred interpretation. In fine, the Open University allows us to rethink the whole question of equality of opportunity, less on the basis of theory and speculation than on the basis of real – and continuing – problems beyond that of open access.

The *Vise Skole*, as we have seen, is the main instrument for catering for part-time education and in particular fulfilling what one might term a recycling function, that is the renewal of skills amongst those already in employment. Recent enrolment figures suggests, however, that this institution is proving less attractive and, for one reason or another, its expansion has been outstripped by the university.

Even so, it is nevertheless apparent that equality of educational opportunity is only one amongst a number of considerations and options that face governments at the present time. For, as we saw in Chapter 4, not all our new structures were conceived to meet this priority. Many of them, the *vise skole*, the IUTs, for instance, were set up with the view of responding to economic demands, of providing skills and training necessary to sustain the general economic development of the country. Others, for instance, the district colleges in Norway combined both educational opportunity and regional development, a task which, unofficially has been identified with the English polytechnics by various private individuals, though officially, their task is one of administrative cost-saving by a more judicious usage of human and physical resources in education. Only the Open University can be said to have developed with equality of educational opportunity as its main justification.

This is not to say that equality of educational opportunity is to be seen in a Manichean light as the total antithesis to manpower planning. For, as we saw in Chapter 7, even those institutes most closely identified with economic priorities attained some measure of greater equality in access to higher education *vis a vis* their university counterparts. But conversely, neither does this mean that manpower planning of necessity involves the automatic creation of more educational opportunity. Indeed, as we pointed out in Chapter 1, it is as possible to meet manpower targets by re-directing students who would, in any case, have continued to higher education, as it is by admitting hitherto excluded groups in society to post-secondary education. Yet, both policies — manpower considerations and equal opportunity — can be justified by mutual reference. For instance, it is possible to argue the necessity for greater equality of educational opportunity in higher education on the utilitarian grounds that to do otherwise would deprive the country of the benefits deriving from the realized abilities of hitherto disadvantaged sectors of the community. And equally, it is possible to justify manpower planning policies on the grounds that the resultant spin off in economic terms will better enable a country to devote itself to the task of realizing social justice in all domains.

But justification is not the same thing as choice between various policy options. Often it is used merely to cloak decisions already taken that might, if revealed in all their nakedness, gain less support from interests threatened by the prospective reform. Choice, however, is precisely the problem facing higher education today. In Chapter 3 we examined some of the forward planning trends and proposals for structural innovation presented by various Western European governments. Most of them revolved around one central issue — the issue of graduate unemployment. Some, though by no means all, sought a solution in terms of a more rigid application of the *numerus clausus*. Others, Denmark and the Netherlands, for instance, envisaged reducing the length of study at the university level and placing more stringent conditions for admission to long course study, whilst, at the same time, offering a more 'comprehensive' spread of short courses for those wishing to change in mid-stream.

The question of graduate saturation cannot, however, be dismissed as being of interest simply to employers, administrators or to the economists. It has immediate repercussions upon the whole strategy of equality of opportunity, not merely in the sector of higher but also in secondary education, since it is from secondary schools that the future graduates come.

In most countries, the secondary sector is itself engaged in far reaching curricular and fundamental structural reforms, associated with the move towards universalizing secondary education; effectively, this means creating equality of educational opportunity in this area of the education system. The imposition of a policy of *numerus clausus*, or selective entry either to university or post-secondary education, subordinates the task of the secondary school to concentrate differentially upon either selecting those students destined for higher education, or devoting extra time to them. (102) Thus, the mechanism of selection in higher education risks upholding those very structures and practices of differentiation historically associated with an élitist model of secondary education precisely at a time when reform is intended to eliminate them.

When we turn our attention to the higher education sector alone, we find equally crucial problems. Un- or underemployment amongst graduates calls into question the whole concept of equality of educational opportunity. All too ofteñ this has been seen in terms of facilitating access for socially deprived groups. Certainly, one can argue that there is an element of equality if the son of the *entrepreneur* shares the dole queue with the bargee's daughter, both brandishing their PhDs. But is this the equality previous definitions of the concept meant?

Of no less importance is the fact that the social and pedagogic consequence of 'graduate saturation' appear scarcely to have been considered by the various countries, with the exception of the Netherlands. It seems almost like a paradox that, in the year when the Sex Discrimination Act finally emerged onto the British statute book, the Manpower Planning Unit in the Department of Employment can contemplate benignly the prospect that 'by 1981 between one and four per cent of *men* graduates and between eighteen and twenty-two per cent of *women* graduates might be employed in jobs not traditionally filled by graduates' (103).

If the consequences of the present economic crisis are not carefully thought through, as much in social and pedagogic terms as in its economic and labour market implications, there is the distinct possibility that the methods of allocation to jobs and hence to social status upheld in an élitist education system will find new favour and justification. Effectively, these methods, deemed mete and just for a society based upon an *a priori* concept of class as a determinant of educability or as a 'neutral' means of identifying 'intelligence' and thus deciding who shall go to higher education — means assured by psychometrical testing — can as easily be justified in the name of economic necessity as they were previously in the name of 'natural selection'.

The lesson which might be drawn from this is that one should not assign rigid distinctions between higher education as the instrument of economic necessity and the secondary school which, gradually, is becoming the instrument for equalizing educational opportunity. In future, educational management will be obliged, to an increasing degree, to espouse an 'ecological' or holistic approach to the whole education system. And this in turn means a further dissolution of the traditionally separate and autonomous systems of secondary and higher education. In short, the process which we see at work blurring the demarcation lines between secondary and primary education extends upward to the link point between secondary and higher education. As the Dutch government noted in its report on future trends '... education in the future will have to be based ... (upon) a redefinition of its social function' (104).

However, a redefinition of the social function of education is not something that can be undertaken simply by dint of legislation, decree or resolution. Certainly, such classic instruments of policy clarification may, to some extent, redefine the framework in which the subsequent re-orientation of values may take place, perhaps sooner, perhaps later, perhaps not at all. This does not mean to say that such steps should not be taken, though ultimately, as we have seen in connexion with the Open University (*vide* Chapter 7), the degree to which educational opportunity may become a reality depends on aspects of social dynamics not readily manipulable by legislative or even by financial methods. No amount of lawgiving will change the way in which an individual perceives his life situation. Nor can it foresee, with any real accuracy how individuals will revise the view they entertain of the various options open to them, in the field of education. Indeed, it is of the essence of Western democracy that individuals be allowed to refuse what other rational men would conceive as being in their best interests. But to be able to refuse means, essentially, having a choice. *What legislation may do, if it is so inclined, is to create the facilities by which choice is possible, either through the setting up of systems involving recurrent education or through the creation of funds – alternatively, vouchers – which adult citizens may use to their perceived advantage.*

But this, in effect, means the creation of an educational structure in which the main role it performs is defined, not so much by governments, as by individuals. The role of governments in this, the individual centred interpretation of educational opportunity, is limited to providing ways and means. How far it is a realistic proposition in the light of the present crisis is, of course, disputable. What is equally disputable are the possible consequences of *not* so doing. As to the effectiveness of such a course of action, we have seen that the structure nearest equivalent to it, namely the Open University, enjoys a far higher 'score' on the index we constructed than any of the other institutions – be they binary, as in the case of the polytechnics, specialized, as in the case of the IUTs and the *Gesamthochschule* or multiple access models, as in the case of the *vise skole* and the Norwegian district colleges. Yet such a suggestion presupposes that equality of educational opportunity is, if not the only consideration, then at least the overriding and primary one.

Assuming for a moment, that this proposition were entertained and, amongst other things, no other considerations were brought into play, it is worthwhile examining some of the implications such a course of action would hold, particularly in the realm of the teaching profession itself. It goes without saying that education, particularly higher education is a 'labour intensive industry'. Furthermore, it is comparatively ill-defined insofar as job specifications are concerned. Teachers are expected both to research and to teach. Some, though by no means all, countries expect them to assume an administrative role as well. Within this perspective, it is axiomatic that any measure introduced to 'democratize' higher education — that is, to open access to disadvantaged groups in society — also means the democratization of the teaching body, that is, the removal of historical distinctions between degree holders, non degree holders, between *agrégés*, PhD and *Habilierten* and *licenciés*, bachelors and those with the *staatsexamen*. Indeed, within an historical perspective this process is inevitably part of the 'industrialization' of higher education. Just as the industrialization of society removed artisan skills and replaced them by skills of a general and interchangeable nature, so the abolition of the distinction between upper degrees — the equivalent of specialized artisans — leads towards the creation of a general — and hence mobile — academic labour force, interchangeable between the 'noble' and 'non-noble' sectors of the higher education system. One can go further with this analogy. The gradual merging of status in the academic world, status derived from the type of study one has undertaken, is itself, the basic prior condition to creating a successful policy of diversification in higher education and even the *sine qua non* of the transition from systems of education based on the concept of autonomy and corporative privilege to a network of mutually interlocking and mutually supporting institutions. To some such a process will appear as the proletarianization of the academic artisanate. To others the same process will doubtless possess the same significance that the abolition of guild privileges in the France of 1792 had for the setting up of a mobile pool of employees.

Yet, if the setting up of a 'network' based system, with horizontal mobility of students between different sectors and courses stands in the same relationship to the university world as the transition from medieval to early industrial work relationships, the Open University carries this one stage further. The outstanding hallmark of the Open University resides in its concentration and centralization of educational resources. Certainly the use of mass media and instantaneous communications enables them to be rapidly diffused *throughout* the population. But the creation of courses, the concentration of personnel, student guidance systems and evaluative instruments in one major centre represents the same stage in the education world as economic development in the time of 'high capitalism'. The economic equivalent to the Open University is, organizationally speaking, the cartel or perhaps even the industrial conglomerate. The advantages are also the same, economies of scale, higher production rates, 'quality control' rather than a reliance on the ingenuity of various artisans each creating, some for better some for worse, their own article — or course, or lecture.

The acceptance of an Open University model therefore, has profound implications for not only the academic labour market, but also for the teaching profession in higher education. Logically, it presents a possibility of the profession splitting into two distinct parts: on the one hand those engaged in higher research to prepare for national courses to be televised or diffused by radio and on the other, the emergence of a large number of para-educational services to assure the back up of the central system. It would be likely that such para-educational services, guidance, orientation, tutorial systems would act as a major employment source for a non-tenured profession. Indeed, *the major bulk of teaching could just as well be assured by part-time tutors etc., releasing the expertise otherwise confined to the university and the non-university world into other areas of the national economy.*

It is obvious, however, that such a system would almost certainly arouse violent hostility on the part of various sectional interests in academia. It is equally evident that the gain derived from rationalization could just as well be nullified by the development of an equally rigid corporation, based not upon teachers' privileges, but on the interests of a para-educational bureaucracy. Yet, one thing is very clear. *It cannot be argued anymore that educational opportunity is better forwarded by either centralized or decentralized systems of education.* One may put forward arguments in defence of either model-arguments about democratic control, about the need for unfettered inquiry outside the censorship of state administration. But if one's basic criterion is the extent to which either model successfully accomplishes equality of educational opportunity, then the formal administrative relationship is totally and utterly irrelevant. *What is relevant, however, is availability of facilities for education, independent of where one resides, works or has one's being.* And total availability means the alliance of two structures in one and the same organization: *central control* to assure a homogeneity of standards, and a *diffusion* which, effectively, breaks the monopoly of education from both its spatial and temporal base. Such availability is not possible in institutions that demand as price of conferring certificates, diplomas and degrees a physical presence. For such methods of attendance *automatically* place in a position of disadvantage those in underpopulated areas, those whose occupation involves extreme and regular fatigue; in short, *so long as availability is conceived in terms of physical institutional availability, any policy attempting to realize equality of educational opportunity will merely unearth those obstacles to learning that are inherent in existing occupational structures without necessarily being able to overcome them.* Such was the conclusion one might draw from the evidence presented in Chapter 7, particularly that related to the Open

University.

In the long run, the philosophic principle that governs any policy forwarding equality of opportunity in education is the elimination as far as possible, of arbitrariness. One may call this the chance factors of birth, family upbringing, environment, occupation and fortune, factors which have inspired some of the most important political and social experiments over the past two centuries, since, in fact the time of the first French Revolution. That their elimination was, then seen in terms of the franchise, of universal suffrage and self-determination merely reflected a faith that institutional reform and legislative methods were sufficient on their own to accomplish the task. The lesson that one might draw from the history, if not from the sociology and psychology of education, is that legislation on its own is not sufficient. Were it so, then the elimination of arbitrariness might well have begun on the night of the 4th of August 1789.

Recommendations for further research

Research which can propose solutions capable of immediate implementation is rare! In most cases, it serves to unearth more problems than those it sets out to understand and perhaps to help pose a solution. This study is no exception. Indeed, it would appear to fall four square into that most indelicate of all categories – research which, like Oliver Twist, has the impudence of asking for 'More'. However, in this brief outline we will show why further research into this area is imperative and, hopefully having proved our case, go on to outline some avenues that might prove particularly fruitful.

Why further research is necessary

Throughout this inquiry two themes have surfaced time and again. The first is the search after alternative forms of higher education apt to realize greater educational opportunity. The second is the enormous gap between what governments intended in their legislative enactments and what in fact emerged in the form of student input of the various institutions legislation created. At a simple level of argument, we need to know how these institutions continue to develop, what the obstacles are to realizing equality of educational opportunity, and what their successes have been. It is certain, for example, that a series of monitoring investigations on an international basis would fulfil several functions. First, they would permit us to gauge the extent to which policies involving structural innovation have or have not been successful. As in any evaluation of a scientific nature, negative results are perhaps in many ways as important as positive ones. And an international study would enable us to see to what extent the problems of development are shared across widely differing institutional types.

Second, it would also allow us to see to what degree different structures departed from one another in their various problems. In short, such monitoring research fulfils a similar function within the framework of higher education as the concept of *education permanente*. Indeed, it is the policymaker's and the administrator's counterpart of recurrent education.

Having stated this, it is immediately apparent that the role of educational research becomes quantitatively and qualitatively more important and necessary as education systems themselves move towards an increasing degree of flexibility both from the standpoint of student choice, curricular content and — as a consequence of these innovations — of their centrality in both social and economic development. Looking at this problem from an historical standpoint, it is probably correct to say that government decision-making *vis a vis* higher education without reference to educational research is possible only in relatively static and / or highly selective and élitist systems of higher education. In such a system research becomes necessary only when there emerges gross malfunctioning and when the government of the day has already taken the decision to implement reform. In highly complex systems dealing with a wide variety of institutions, each containing a veritable plethora of different levels of course, modes of study, and conditions of access, research performs two well-defined functions. First, that of providing straight information on the development of such systems, information that may be used to carry out minor corrections of a routine administrative nature. Second, that of undertaking periodically a fundamental evaluation with a view to assisting in further innovation or to search for more efficacious forms of institution.

1. *Monitoring research*

Most of the institutions we examined in the course of this study are of relatively recent foundation. Some, for instance, the district colleges have only just emerged from their experimental status. Others, for instance, the *Gesamthochschule* Kassel are still in this situation. Further studies in this area should at least permit an assessment of their achievements over time and thus contribute to a greater understanding of the possible alternative models that one might derive from their experience. Studies on this aspect might well use the present investigation as a blueprint or template.

2. *Wider international comparisons*

Perhaps one of the most fruitful areas of research would be an investigation designed to assess the consequences upon the equality of educational opportunity of the *absence* of new structures in a country's system of higher education. In effect, by choosing those countries where such institutions exist, we have adopted the belief that new structures do make a difference. And, within their respective nations such a difference is visible when compared to the university sector. Nevertheless, by the very nature of the design and the remit of this investigation we have had to exclude what one might term — following the jargon of the statistician — the null hypothesis, namely that from the standpoint of systems performance, the presence of new structures do not have any appreciable effect on the degree of equality attained.

3. *Effect of structural innovation upon insertion into the labour force*

As we have seen, one of the objectives of many of our target institutions — polytechnics, *vise skole*, IUTs, district colleges, and the *Gesamthochschule* Kassel — is the creation of courses designed to assist their graduates to find employment in the developing sectors of the economy in their respective countries. At a time of considerable unemployment amongst young people generally throughout the Community, it is obviously paramount that this aspect of the new structures be ascertained, evaluated and assessed. There are, not unnaturally other reasons that one might advance in support of such investigations. The principle reasons are two: First, the new structures represent a considerable investment on the part of their governments. Second, the whole notion of educational innovation can only be justified, at least from the manpower planner's point of view, so long as it has the effect legislation and investment claimed, namely the provision of skills outside those normally associated with the classical university. Such a study should perhaps not limit itself to investigating the student flow to particular sectors of industry, commerce and administration, but should also ascertain the degree of job mobility of individuals graduating from the various institutions in higher education.

It should, of course, be pointed out that very few of such studies have been carried out into this aspect of the new structures. Those that have, are more often than not, limited to individual institutions. Hence, important though this area is, any future project would require a considerable degree of field work on a national basis — perhaps even sample surveying — before it could proceed to any meaningful analysis of the international dimension.

4. *Student decision making vis a vis the new structures*

One area which we have touched upon in this investigation, but which lends itself to further examination is the decision making process of students proceeding either from secondary education or from the world of work into the new structures. National statistics will, of course, give us some indication of the differences in educational background, but, interesting as this is, we need to know more about how such structures are perceived by students *before* they enter. In short, we need to know more about the motivation factors that prompt school leavers to choose this type of institution for positive reasons, rather than as a *pis aller*. Retrospective research carried out on the basis of examining students once they are in such institutions is somewhat suspect, methodologically speaking. It is, after all the easiest thing in the world to give positive reasons for entering such establishments if, for instance, one has failed to gain a place at university. But if one takes such reasons as their face value, as many of the studies into this domain are apt to do, our planning — not to mention our understanding of the rise of these institutions — is based on myth. We also need to know when the decision is made in the individual's career and what were the influences exerted upon him or her to choose one rather than another sector of higher education. If such aspects as these are not taken into account, then there is the very real possibility that institutions which start out as ventures in innovation become ventures in social segregation, instruments of further social stratification and devises supporting the justification of a differentiated approach to higher education.

5. In an area of the education system undergoing rapid change, both as regards student inflow, curricular development and evolving conditions of access, it is important that an overall view be maintained. Research undertaken within the framework of individual countries should have a more rapid inflow into the monitoring function. To this end we recommend that a facility for researchers to meet for discussion of findings, exchange of information etc., be created either in the form of a conference or in the shape of a working group with the specific remit to keep abreast of developments in this domain.

6. There is finally the question of what is known technically as 'permeability' that is the possibility of flows between various sectors of higher education, between for instance, the university sector and the non-traditional forms of higher education, new structures included. It is desirable that an inquiry be undertaken to ascertain the characteristics as well as the extent to which transfer facilities between different forms of institution are used by students, what the educational and social characteristics of the students are who avail themselves of such facilities and their motivation for undertaking this move. In a system of higher education in which traditional forms exist alongside non-traditional patterns, a sector by sector study is no longer of any particular help. For essentially such sectorial studies have, as their fundamental assumption, the non-permeability of their component institutions. In various points throughout this investigation, we have stressed the

development of what has been termed a 'network approach' to the problems of higher education, such an approach being fully in keeping with the development of higher education itself. Those students who move from one sector to another in higher education are, to use an apocryphal phrase, the shape of things to come. Hence, if we are to understand *now* the ramifications of the type of education systems we are establishing for tomorrow, it is as well to gain some insight into those who, today, are already taking advantage of the new flexibility we have created.

In a more specific framework, however, there are certain statistical indicators which should be incorporated into any study of the nature which we have outlined above. Recommendations in this direction are made below.

Recommendations for social indicators for assessing equality of educational opportunity

The recommendations presented here for the gathering of additional statistical information are of two kinds: first, those which, had they existed, would have rendered the inquiry more rapid and more conclusive; second, those which, had they been placed on an international and comparable basis would have facilitated it considerably.

1. *Application patterns on an individual basis to various types of post secondary education.*

One feature common to the various policies for realizing greater educational opportunity is the creation of greater diversity in post-secondary education. Greater diversity means, in effect, greater choice, more complex decision making. Only in a few instances, for example, in-depth studies of student flows, do we know the type of institution to which students applied. Most national statistics give information on application patterns by sector, that is those who applied to universities only, or those who applied to regional colleges. This methodology is justifiable so long as each sector is autonomous and contains specific and differentiated levels of study. Degree courses in university, non-degree courses in district colleges, for instance. Where there is a considerable overlap in study level between institutions, we are faced with an evolving network system of higher education, and possibly, greater choice. We need to know the application patterns of individuals for the following reasons:

a. educational opportunity is measured not only by the number of *entrants* to higher education, but also by the number of *applicants*.

b. *Changes in individual application patterns to higher education often presage a shift in short-term demand for higher education.* Without this data, basic planning policy is apt to be nullified by sudden, unforeseen upsurges or down turns in 'demand'. The economic consequence of this needs no further elaboration.

c. Elitist definitions of educational opportunity dwell upon the notion of 'a pool of ability'. This ability is defined not so much by the individual in relation to his perceived 'need for education', as by the education system, which is itself a generator of and contributor to, inequality. To define demand in terms of the proportion of those 'qualified' i.e., holders of the School Leaving Certificate — is thus vastly to underestimate the extent of 'hidden demand'. For *no system can pretend to equality of educational opportunity when its resources are lavished upon those who are successful in it.* This is not to say that an education system which excludes certain people from post-school and higher education is inegalitarian. There is obviously a limit to the amount of money a country's, or for that matter, a community's education budget may claim, and thus to the number of people it can sustain in institutes of learning, training and reskilling. But that limit is more precisely ascertained by defining 'demand' on a basis of individual need as expressed by application, regardless of the level of qualification an individual holds rather than by the successive and accumulative certification imposed at the ages of 17 to 21.

2. *Distinction between direct and indirect first time entrants*

Throughout this investigation, we have tried to draw a line between direct and indirect entrants. We have suggested that the trends towards an individual centred interpretation of educational opportunity is characterized by the emergence of a 'non sequential relationship' between secondary and higher education. We have seen the extent to which it has developed in the case of the Open University, for example. By direct entrant we mean those who enter higher education directly from school. By 'indirect' entry we mean those entering after a period of full time gainful employment. This criterion variable becomes increasingly important as higher education systems adapt to the notion of recurrent education or *education permanente*. Indeed, without its monitoring, *education permanente* is deprived of one of its primary evaluative instruments. However, we need to draw a distinction between those students whose employment since leaving school is in the nature of 'short term temporary status' and those who come from permanent occupations.

a. *Direct entrants*, those coming to higher education for the first time within less than a year of leaving secondary school.

b. *Indirect entrants*, those coming to higher education for the first time having been employed full time for two years or more. Obviously, it is as inaccurate to classify students entering higher education from military service or VSO as indirect as it would be to classify a person entering higher education after a period of two years unemployment as a direct entrant. On the other hand, it is possible that to classify such persons on the basis of having held a *particular* job for two years would exclude large numbers of young adults at a time when inter-job mobility is at its highest.

    c. As a subdivision of this group, one should perhaps draw a distinction between those entering higher education *viz* university, polytechnics, IUT who gained additional qualifications on a part-time basis in another type of institute in the post-secondary sector. This is an important trend, of which account should be taken, particularly in the UK where there is an increasing tendency for school leavers to continue study in a college of further education either on part- or full-time basis, in order to enter, subsequently, higher education. If they enter the post-secondary sector directly from school prior to entry to university, such students constitute *Second Route Entrants*.

    d. The justification for this new system of classifying student flows into higher education may be found amongst the reasons advanced in support of data on individual application patterns; namely, the development of 'network' systems of higher education, whether in the form of multiple access models such as we see in the *vise skole* or in the form of the comprehensive university. Simply to group first year students on an institutional level as 'First time entrants' tells nothing whatsoever about their previous educational background, still less is it a useful method of evaluating the impact of 'network' systems either upon the economy or upon the occupational structure.

3. The measurement of 'throughput'

    Most systems of higher education possess some information on the wastage rates at university level. This is generally held to be in the region of 15 per cent at the end of a three year course at English universities, around 60 per cent in France and approximately 20 to 25 per cent in Scotland. In the case of the Open University study we saw how the throughput rate varied according to the various qualification levels students held on entry. Obviously, *if equality of educational opportunity is to have any meaning it cannot be confined to measuring differences in the 'student input', that is to say, access to higher education. One has also to attend to the 'output'*, unless, that is, equality is equality in the sense of permitting equal possibilities of failure to larger numbers of entrants to higher education. With the exception of the IUTs we know relatively little about the 'through put' rates for institutions providing 'university level' study which are not formally recognized as being in a university, for example, the polytechnics, the regional colleges, or the *Gesamthochschulen*, though in the case of the two latter institutions, their experimental nature and the relatively short time they have operated precludes this for several years. *Simply to measure the number of diplomas, degree certificates awarded in any one year is not particularly satisfying, nor is it a particularly accurate indicator.* It is not satisfying because 'output' in terms of absolute numbers of certificates in a given year can comprise the simultaneous 'certification' of widely different entry cohorts. In one year, therefore, certificates issued are the sum of those courses which ended in that year, but which began, however, at different points in time, some two, others three or more years ago. Hence, it is not particularly accurate either.

a. *The measurement of cohort throughput* is necessary as systems of higher education become more complex and as length of study itself becomes diversified.

b. It is also an important indicator in changes in student behaviour especially when institutions permit, as they do to an increasing extent, the pattern of following short modules of study without completing the full course. Recent development, in Sweden, for example, seems to point to the growth of 'dropping in' for one or two credits, rather than remaining for the full 'stretch'. How far this is also true in other 'new structures' of higher education is still somewhat of a mystery, though it is reasonable to conclude that, in general, it is becoming more widespread. Hence, such an indicator is an important instrument in evaluating the development of education systems, not merely from the economist's standpoint — in terms of gross investment as against graduates produced or overproduced — but also the extent to which those systems are adapting to different demand patterns for varying length of courses.

4. *Standardized classification of social and occupational status*

Future estimates on the degree to which various EEC countries are managing to assure equality of educational opportunity in higher education will depend on devising a standardized classification system for social class and occupational status. And this, in turn, demands that member countries make regular surveys into this aspect. Some, the French and German governments already have this provision. Others, for instance, the UK have only partial information on particular sectors. For example, this information is available for the universities through the Statistical Supplements of the Universities Central Council on Admissions Reports. It is not available for polytechnics, partly because of their decentralized nature. The standardization of occupational status is not, technically a difficult operation. The OECD already has such a system and, with suitable programming modifications, it can be provided by any reasonable statistical service.

5. Problems of accuracy and 'false returns'

There is finally the question of accuracy of returns. The more complex an education system, the greater the amount of duplication in study levels between different institutional types, the greater the possibility of inaccuracies. Nor should one forget the fact that many returns are made merely to prove that a particular institution is fulfilling its mission *vis a vis* the public.

What Can Britain Learn from Current European Developments?

'Who knows if that which appears true today will seem so thirty years hence or will appear so to men of another century'.

Pierre Bayle, *Commentaire Philosophique*, Rotterdam, 1686.

In some respects, the very strength of the cross-national study in education policy is its major weakness. Though it provides a yardstick against which national developments may be measured, its conclusions, culled from differing countries, are applicable to no one nation. In one sense, this is as it should be. In another, it is a very tedious convention, pleasing everyone, as it was once said of an interdenominational Prayer Book, but offensive to God. In this study, we hope to get the best of both worlds by adding to the general conclusion a postscript which asks one specific question: 'What can Britain learn from current European developments?'

That this question is especially relevant at the present time, none can doubt. The effect of the economic crisis and the cuts back in educational finance and budgeting at all levels, and in most EEC countries, has been to raise once again, the Aunt Sally of equality of educational opportunity versus manpower planning needs. That these are seen as mutually exclusive issues begs more questions about our capacity to learn from previous experience than it helps in solving current problems. As we pointed out in Chapter 1 and again in Chapter 8, the two issues may be seen separately. But the decision to separate them on an either / or basis suggests that they are not viewed by governments as interactive. In other words, too often it is supposed that, in England, if one's goals involve equality of educational opportunity, they can only be attained at the expense of deserting the imperative needs of the economy. Thus, if one's needs are construed in terms of more engineers − let us say − then this priority automatically rules out strategies in higher education designed to overcome the inequalities in secondary education. In fact, British educationists and planners can learn from this study that, for a particular type of institution to subscribe to the priority of manpower needs, does not exclude its creating greater equality of educational opportunity at the same time. This we saw both in the case of the Yugoslavian two year college (*vise skole*) and also in the case of the Norwegian district colleges (or, as they are now to be known, study centres).

In this study we have been dealing mainly with institutions outwith the university sector, institutions which, in the main, were conceived in terms of providing middle range technical and technological *cadres*, and management. In Britain, by contrast, the current debate today centres around the question of high level technological manpower and in particular, the question of adequately trained and scientifically based management for industry. The difference is, in short, one of degree. In this conclusion we shall look at some of the broader implications that arise from our investigation in the context of various solutions proposed in the UK as remedies to this situation. These include the potential as well as the actual importance of the Open University, the notion of 'transformational capacity' as an educational indicator, the status of the British engineer, the notion of 'the reserved graduate occupation', the shortcomings of the 'binary policy' in higher education in England and Wales, and finally the inescapable interdependence of all sectors of a modern education system, élite values in government administration, and the world of work.

1. *The Open University as a radical factor in the promotion of equality of educational opportunity*

Sick man of Europe or not, Britain can take comfort that the Open University takes the European lead as a radical departure from traditional structures in higher education. In seeking to estimate the degree to which various institutions included in this study contributed to advancing equality of educational opportunity, we constructed an index on which the Open University scored nearly four times higher than any other institution investigated. This index consisted of the following items:

a. The proportion of students in a given type of institution aged 25 plus;

b. The proportion of students following degree level courses who were not formally qualified;

c. The proportion of working class students in a given type of institution.

It can, quite reasonably, be argued that such an index measures only the degree to which various types of institution provide *access* to higher education for disadvantaged groups in society. This is true. Equally, however, it should be remembered that, prior to the present crisis, equality of educational opportunity was defined mainly in terms of student access rather than in terms of student output. That our perspective is changing reflects not only the changed climate of the times, but also the need to bring qualifications closer in line with what are thought to be *lacunae* in the skills demanded for economic recovery. Yet if we change our perspective on educational opportunity, we must change also our perspective on that other issue which is often seen as the ineluctable concomitant to casting down the historical restrictions for entry to higher education: namely 'standards'.

Some will argue that, by admitting formally unqualified students, the new structures are indulging in intellectual treason, academic turpitude and scholarly spinelessness. Hence, they will conclude, policies for equalizing educational opportunity do — objectively — bring about a fall in standards. However, the definition of what constitutes 'standards' depends — like the notion of equality against which it inveighs — upon equality defined in terms of *access*. Once equality is defined in terms of student *output*, then so also must standards be redefined similarly. What matters at that point is not the qualifications — or lack of qualifications — of students entering new structures, so much as their characteristics, capacities and qualifications when they leave them. In other words, by concentrating on the student output, new structures being about two significant changes in our concepts about both equality and manpower planning. In the first place, it suggests that, from an institutional standpoint, the degree to which one particular institution fulfils the goal of equality depends on which might be termed its 'transformational capacity,' a concept not dissimilar to the economist's notion of the value added function.

2. Transformational capacity: the concept can be applied to manpower planning

The idea of 'transformational capacity' is central to the argument and it is appropriate to spent a little time elaborating it. Prior to the 1960s — a period commonly identified with the élitist phase in the development of higher education in Europe — (see Chapter 1), the transformational capacity of higher education was narrow and limited. The educational function of the post-war university was to provide highly able students whose ability had been proven by public examination, to reach a more or less common standard after a stipulated period of time. This standard was usually equated with the first degree. In fine, degree standards depended on having a high level of input in terms of the educational characteristics of the individual entrant. In this context, one can best appreciate the notion of 'transformational capacity': simply, the higher the initial ability range and educational characteristics of entrants to a particular type of institution, the narrower and more restricted the strategies needed to 'transform' that individual up to a particular standard — in this case, degree level. By contrast, the wider and more diverse the qualifications of individual entrants, the greater must be the transformational capacity of the institution to bring some of them to degree standard. Thus, if we examine this conceptual tool in terms of specific instances, it is not obvious that the transformational capacity from input to degree level is greater amongst polytechnics than universities. But it is very obvious that it is greater within the Open University.

In this connexion too, it is not without importance to note the exceptional performance of the Open University. We saw in Chapters 6 and 7 that the OU was conceived mainly as a device for realizing greater equality in access to higher education. That it has a greater transformational capacity is not without importance for manpower planning considerations, even though they did not form the basis for its creation. The greater the transformational capacity, the greater the possibility of the institution's ability to respond to manpower needs, on a relatively short term basis. It is, consequently, not inconceivable, for example, that the OU could act, if it were so to be required, as an extremely effective vehicle for the emergency training of mathematics teachers.

3. *Relevance of the investigation of current proposals for future educational policy*:

Once again, the current issue in the education world is focused on manpower planning. The daily breast beating, lamentation and liturgy among polytechnic directors, vice chancellors, from heads of nationalized industries and from eminent scientists about the lowly status of the spurned 'engineer' is not new. It has, rather, returned to the headlines of fashion after several years lying fallow; to be precise, since the publication of the Swann and Dainton reports in 1966 and 1968 on the flow of scientific manpower into industry and the flow of scientists and technologists into higher education. If then, the cause for concern was the decline in the number of students following science courses at school and at university, today the perspective has altered somewhat. Now, as our eyes are turned towards Europe, the 'Auld Lament' grows greater. The specifically *British Disease*, diagnosed by Professor Allen, is that men (*sic*) educated in vocational or professional subjects were seldom elevated to the ranks of policy makers. A less subtle observer, such as the Director of Huddersfield Polytechnic, notes merely that the economies of France and Germany are in better shape than that of Britain. From this he draws some prescriptive conclusions from the fact that their Engineers are educated in non-university institutions, such as the *Technische Hochschulen* and the *Grandes Ecoles*.[1] Arguments such as the latter often have been produced to support educational innovations of a dubious usefulness as a supposed means of solving the nation's economic ills. Lord Annan, for example, has urged the importation of the *Grandes Ecoles* structures into this country. Imperial College, London — home of engineering as a university subject in Britain — aims at expanding its social science teaching. And finally, more serious because more costly, the Secretary of State for Industry has recently proposed the lure of additional financial incentives for first degree students on courses 'of particular relevance to industrial competitiveness and to the economy.'

All these approaches, whether the 'institutional change' or curriculum revision — even financial inducement — are within the tried and accepted wisdom in this domain. Indeed, the creation of a new type of institution to solve a problem that older types of institution appear unable to do, has lain behind the establishment not merely of the polytechnics, but also of the conversion of colleges of advanced technology into technological universities. If the importation of the French *Grandes Ecoles* is being bruited abroad and about as a means of alleviating the shortage of qualified engineers, then one is forced to admit that the previous institutional solutions have not yet yielded the expected results. If institutional solutions — of which the 50 / 50 split of students between polytechnics and universities is a magnificent illustration — have not met the demands of the country's manpower, what reason is there for thinking that another episode based on similar reasoning and assumptions will prove any the better? Surely, what one learns from the partial success of such policies is that one does not repeat the same error thrice?

This cross European study tends to show that one cannot look to new structures in higher education *on their own* any more than one can look to old structures *on their own* to furnish particular types of graduate manpower. It is, in short, becoming increasingly evident that policies for making higher education more 'efficient' in terms of its qualified output — or to use our own concept, to maximize the transformational capacity of higher education — cannot rely on the single solution. We cannot castigate higher education for problems that

---

1   To believe, let alone state, that the *Technische Hochschulen* or the *Grandes Ecoles*, are non-university institutions and thus to equate them with polytechnics by implication, is nonsense. The former are technical universities, the latter, both as regards entry conditions and standing, are far above the French university in the hierarchy of institutions.

are located elsewhere in the economy, in government and in society generally. In short, if a better quality of 'engineer' is to be made available to industry, the secondary school on the one hand and the administrative civil service on the other, must cease to discriminate against the able person with a bent in that direction.

We suggest that there are two areas of national importance that should be reformed simultaneously. The higher education system itself lies athwart different sectors of the social system; between the labour market on the one hand and the secondary school on the other. In our earlier study, *How they Fared: the impact of the comprehensive school upon the university*, we showed how the maintained secondary school, traditionally, has discriminated against the able student who wanted to follow a 'mixed' combination of subjects i.e. arts, science and technology. This discrimination has taken the form of making timetabling difficult or obliging the student to opt for subject groups he did not wish to take and perhaps forcing him or her to drop out of school earlier than might otherwise have been the case. The earlier study showed too that schools often required pupils to opt prematurely for either arts or sciences when they would rather have kept their options open. Many of these students, faced with the need to choose, opted for arts or for social science combinations which then effectively closed the route to a university science or technology degree. Thus, when Professor R.V. Jones — justifiably — questions the 'Demand Model' by which the extra university arts and social science places and faculty posts were allocated in the post-Robbins university — and polytechnic — expansion, he is putting his finger only on part of the problem. His accusation that it is the 'natural tendency' for the rump of the student body to go for soft options is not in any manner born out by our survey of students who entered university from comprehensive schools. Moreover, we have every reason to believe that the increase in the numbers of 'mixed subject students' now entering university via the comprehensive schools more accurately reflect the wish of the greater body of secondary school pupils in general. Many are now better able to follow their interest in vocationally relevant mathematical, scientific and technological combinations of subjects. But perhaps many others can do so only by dropping out of school early and re-entering the world of study via further education or trades union-sponsored institutions.

This is not to argue that the courses pupils would prefer are always what is right for the economy. Lord Crowther Hunt's assertion that 'natural demand' for various sorts of subjects and places could be manipulated upwards or downwards according to the needs of society, remains both empirically and morally valid. We note simply that some of the changes that manpower planners regard as desirable seem to be taking place already by dint of structural change in reorganized secondary schools; changes that permit greater pupil choice. In short, there is probably more talent for, and interest in, the technological field among many qualified school leavers than emerges from the statistics on subject choice, be they fifth formers, sixth formers or university applicants.

The partial solution is not, however, to tinker either with the education of engineers or to alter the administrative structures of the institutions in which they are educated. This is as futile as fiddling with the tap once the source has run dry, as we argued in *How They Fared*. Rather the problem is to create those conditions both in school — and in society at large — which are conducive to increasing the supply. If the tap is dry and the stopcock fully open, a sensible policy is to see what is in the reservoir. Rushing around with buckets and loud cries of distress may be an impressive activity. But it is scarcely an adequate remedy.

Still, it cannot be emphasized sufficiently that this factor alone does not account for the dearth of sufficient scientific manpower in the UK. Another and one that similarly, lies outside the system of higher education is what many have called the 'disillusion with science'. Others simply attribute it — despairingly — to that mysterious entity — the 'spirit of the times'. Yet, whatever the image of the scientists, of the engineer, that image is a reflection of the power, status, prestige and social standing that such individuals enjoy in our society. And, however distorted that image, it derives nonetheless from social reality. Engineers in the UK do not, for instance, enjoy the standing their German and French colleagues bask in. And this, in turn, derives from the conditions laid down by custom in recruiting to what we call the 'reserved occupations'. We shall return to this later.

4. *Transformational capacity and graduate technological manpower:*
The UK's insufficiency of highly trained and very able scientific and technological manpower can be analysed, as we suggested, in terms of transformational capacity. As we have said, this concept which we used here initially to make a cross national comparison between various new structures of higher education in Europe and their contribution to reducing inequality of opportunity, can also be applied just as easily to the manpower arena. The question we should be asking is 'Why has the UK's educational, social and economic system failed to "transform" enough of its able young people into able young engineers as numerous, proportionately, and as well equipped to be captains of industry as say — able young American, French, Russian and German engineers?'. There is, however, the correlative question. Indeed, it is certainly of equal, if not of more, importance. Still using the concept of

'transformational capacity', we should, then, pose the additional question: 'Why does the educational, social and economic system of the UK still "transform" such a high proportion of its most able young people into graduate philosophers, historians and social scientists?'

Both here and elsewhere, we have pointed to the failure of the selective secondary school to permit, encourage — let alone oblige — enough of its able pupils to follow mixed arts / science / technology combinations of subjects at a sufficiently higher level. Nor should we be astounded either by the secondary school's failure, or by the student's behaviour. No pupil with the precocious ambition of becoming a member of society's governing élite is likely to be without the drive to develop skills in the social, historical, political, economic and moral sciences. To be obliged at an early age to opt for *either* arts *or* science *or* social science in order to secure a university place puts very great pressure on pupils with such an ambition to elect for an arts rather than for a science specialization.

Nevertheless, to reform the school syllabus — to incorporate compulsory mathematics and science — while not reforming simultaneously the entrance examination to the administrative grade of the civil service, would prove only partially effective as a method of producing more graduate engineers. Reform based on a single line of attack is not sufficient, as we intimated earlier. If, for example, it were directed simply at syllabus reform in the school, the likely effect would be simply to push the tendency for potential civil service candidates to opt for arts and social sciences in higher education and still leave a plethora of unfilled places in engineering departments. Or, failing that, for them to be filled by applicants of relatively low ability, not to mention lower political ambition or consciousness. Quite under-standably, the prospect is one of despair and frustration for the highly qualified teaching and research staff that currently maintain those departments. Yet, for all the sound and fury, it is still within the conventional wisdom to argue that industry lacks able engineers because engineers in Britain lack the status of their continental counterparts. Furthermore, it is fully in keeping with the lamentations of educational pundits that in the UK, engineers are supposed to be 'on tap, but never on top'; and that, as a consequence, the profession attracts more the middle management mechanic than the *entrepreneur* who is 'going places'.

5. The 'reserved graduate occupations'

Where we depart from this Babylonian chorus is, however, in our analysis of the reasons for the situation. We need to know why the graduate engineering department fails to attract more able recruits. It is not sufficient simplistically to suggest that this has anything to do with the erosion of the 'profit motive' in private industry. The problem of suitable recruitment to and quality of, the engineers was as much a concern to Lyon Playfair, Professor of Chemistry at Edinburgh University, during the 1860s and to Lord Haldane during the first decade of the century as it is to professors and vice chancellors today. Yet it would be ludicrous to suggest that the profit motive then was not held in any but the highest esteem. Indeed, it is probable that the opposing motives of challenge on the one hand and security of relatively lucrative employment on the other (at least till age 65), is what attracts able persons to compete for key posts in the public domains. Certainly, it has never been established that either high salary or low taxation has any connexion with the propensity to undertake study, to work long hours, to excell at problem solving or to seek status and prestige. How condescending of securely tenured dons and insecurely tenured Cabinet Ministers alike to suggest that students of engineering courses are motivated more by considerations of pelf than the normal run of mankind.

However, to pursue this analysis further, we need to introduce a new notion which we term the concept of the 'reserved graduate occupation'. There was a day when this term might have been coterminous with the notion of the 'professions': the Law, the Church and the Army. If the occupations have changed, their defining characteristics have not. Professional persons have, by dint of their particular education and training, access to certain 'reserved occupations' of high status, security of tenure and high pay guaranteed by the law of the land. Their status follows from the fact that they themselves control the policy of the community and determine its values. Their security follows from the fact that they control entry to their 'occupation' as well as expulsion from it. Furthermore, the state guarantees to a substantial proportion of their members, administrative posts, once termed 'sinecures' which carry with them, as we have said, social power, tenure, salary and status, if not always esteem. Over the past century, world society has seen an increase in the professional groups which have secured access to 'reserved occupations' for their members — clerks to bishoprics, barristers to the judiciary, doctors to Health Service consultancies, etc. In consequence, we would argue, this has improved the status of such groups. Medicine, economic planning, university teaching and research are all accorded reserved occupational status by the state.

Yet, the 'super reserved occupations' of the 20th century polity are, of course, the permanent Civil Service corps, itself exercising supreme control over behaviour and values including, to some degree, control over other 'reserved occupations'. What places are set aside specifically for graduate engineers and scientists in the British system and how does this compare with the different networks in various European countries? This question is not easily answered. Is the engineer the specialist brought in to install the computer or the central heating? Or is the engineer the scientific generalist who puts together technological solutions in a political or industrial context? Different countries put different interpretations, overtones, undertones and connotations upon the very meaning of the word 'engineer.' In France, the *polytechnicien* – the engineer civil servant is at the top of the profession. He has had to sit a rigorous competitive examination which, often, takes two or more years to prepare after the Baccalauréat – or 18 plus. Thus, he has to pass through a series of competitive examinations of increasing difficulty which set him aside for that sort of technical / administrative training.

In the UK, the engineer who moves out of local government, penetrates the central administration from below, rarely, if ever, reaching beyond the middle grade. In France, by contrast, the engineering based administrator penetrates the network of central government from above, from the *Grandes Ecoles* and from that apex of all educational establishments, the *Ecole Polytechnique*. The X (the network of *ex polytechniciens* as it is popularly called) provides a coordination that carries across not only different Ministeries, but also in the case of individuals managing to purchase themselves or be purchased by private firms, out of state administration, into the private sector as well. This network provides, both on an official as well as on a highly important un-official level, that interface between government and industry, not to mention that vital interface between universities, government and industry as well. In short, such a network stands to reinforce precisely those links between university and the nation that seem, in the opinion of many industrialists, as much as professors, scientists as much as engineers – to be the weak point in the UK.

The lesson from this is not, however, that what Britain requires is the educational equivalent of the *Ecole Polytechnique*. That, in typical English fashion, is to mistake the institution for the substance. Nor is it even that. What is required is that entry conditions to the Civil Service be changed so that they discriminate in favour of the generally educated scientist who has political and administrative talent; in short – the continental concept of 'the engineer'. At present such a person is produced only by chance in the British context – and in very small numbers.

With the will to change, the reform might be both simple and far reaching. For would those who have the social consciousness to want to join the élite administrative corps *per se* and who have the ability and tenacity to succeed in a competitive examination experience serious difficulty in absorbing the appropriate scientific and technologically oriented disciplines, provided they be made available at school? It is not a question of 'bringing in the engineers'. We do that already and it has little 'spin off' for industry. It is rather a question of redefining an appropriate general education so that scientists and technological skills are an integral part of it. To adopt an oriental analogy — we should not seek to change the fish but rather the water in which they swim and from which they derive their nourishment.

In short, we refer to the need to reform the structure and conditions of entry to an outmoded and value entrenched body in the value making corps itself — the Civil Service. Only if that reform were undertaken and appropriately implemented would it have the necessary impact on the higher and secondary education systems of the UK. Just imagine the reaction of every headteacher, every university professor and even vice chancellor in the UK, if it were decreed tomorrow that, five years hence, the Civil Service examinations would be open only to candidates who had reached joint honours degree standard in at least one mathematical or scientific or technological subject. Under such circumstances, it is highly unlikely that any sixth former or institution of higher education would delay very long in making the necessary adjustments to curriculum and teaching.

In many ways, as it is conceived at present, the Civil Service entrance examination resembles that curious university television quiz show which allows — purely by coincidence — historians and classicists to shine, but scientists, save the odd question here and there, to suggest impartiality, to appear as uncouth boors. If the flood of history and economics graduates is kept high, it is because that is the path of educational righteousness that leads to the high prestige and 'reserved occupations' at the top of which is the Civil Service. This suggests that educational solutions on their own are neither sufficient nor entirely necessary. To attract high quality recruits requires that one give those rewards which, in the past, have attracted such people. And that, in turn, means opening the Whitehall version of Circe's Garden to the Odysseus-like crew of engineers, technologists and scientists.

One may, even so, argue that were this step taken, it would demand ten or twenty years for the technologically trained administrator to move into the upper ranks. Furthermore, as educationists will point out, the English education system, highly specialized, is unable to switch the high ability school leaver with arts qualifications into the necessary grounding for training in applied sciences. Against this one can present two points. Let us deal with the educational objection first of all. There is, as we noted earlier, a growing tendency for school leavers — and especially those in comprehensive schools — to mix their A-levels in a combination of science and non-science subjects. Since many of them are of high ability and, in addition, have the possibility of choosing between arts, sciences and social sciences at university and polytechnic, here is a fruitful source of students who, were the barriers removed from Civil Service entry that favoured arts and social science students, might be attracted into engineering and applied science studies. In other words, the educational obstacles are not as great as one might think, particularly if the trend towards the mixed subject student continues.

The second point is rather more subtle. It involves what one might term the 'spin off' from the creation of competitive admission to high status 'reserved occupations'. As with any competitive examination – and the Civil Service entrance is a very nice illustration here – by definition not all applicants are successful. It is indeed, true to say that the majority are not successful. The question is, 'What happens to those who "fail" this examination or, having been prepared for it, decide not to sit?' The answer is that they go into commerce, teaching, industry, management, advertising, journalism, law, Parliament, even trades union administration. That the optimum educational background for success in the Civil Service examination is currently either history, languages or social sciences means that those occupations are impregnated by people with similar fundamental disciplines.

Assuming such people have their own equivalents of the French X – call it the 'Old Boy Network' or the 'Old College Scarf', that means that the essential interface between government and industry, between university, government and private enterprise, is still assured by mean and women of talent. But in Britain currently, an improperly large proportion of sub-Civil Service graduate manpower – from Prime Ministers downwards, is assured by people of a literary or a social scientific formation not, as in France, by persons of a scientific or a technological discipline.

The British Secretary of State for Industry, Eric Varley, has noticed that the qualifications for top managers in Britain seem to be an Oxbridge Arts degree topped with some management education (*Times Higher Education Supplement*, July 23rd, 1976, p. 5). We suggest that Table 9.2 shows fairly conclusively why young people with ambition to hold top jobs (salary scales going up to £20,175 for a permanent secretary), are right to suppose they have a greater chance if they opt for arts subjects at university. It also explains why hundreds of able graduates but with an arts background are launched into the sub-Civil Service professions every year.

The reversal of the present ratio of 80–20 in favour of arts and social science entrants to the Civil Service within the administrative grade would, we suggest, be likely to have an effect far beyond the portals of St James. If the central administration were able to undertake such an enterprise, the consequence of it would be to shift

Table 9.1: Field of university study previously followed by successful graduate entrants to the Administrative Grade of the British Civil Service 1971–1975* (percentages)

SUBJECT	1971	1972	1973	1974	1975
Education	0.5	0.4	0	0	0
Medical Studies	0	0	0	0.3	0
Engineering / Technology	1.5	3.4	1.3	1.0	1.5
Agriculture, Veterinary studies, Forestry		0	0	0.3	0
Science / Mathematics	10.7	13.9	16.4	11.9	16.3
Social Sciences	33.5	28.5	25.2	29.0	28.9
of which Economics	7.7	6.3	5.6	5.2	7.9
Architecture etc.	0	0	0	0	0.3
Languages	27.9	25.2	31.9	29.4	26.2
of which Classics	6.1	5.4	7.5	8.4	4.9
Arts other than Languages	29.9	24.1	24.6	28.1	26.6
of which History	27.9	23.1	18.6	22.6	22.4
Number	197	238	317	310	263

* Source: derived from *Civil Service Recruitment of Graduates 1974 and 1975*, London, Civil Service Commission, Table 13.

Table 9.2: Absolute Numbers of successful and unsuccessful applicants (1974) according to the degree subject followed at university

In 1974, 18.7 per cent of all candidates for the Administrative Trainee grade (not including HM Inspectors of Taxes) were accepted. If we make the assumption that this proportion of successful applicants of all who applied did not vary between different fields of degree subject, we can estimate the number of unsuccessful applicants who would be forced, possibly, into top jobs.

SUBJECT	All applicants	Those unsuccessful	Those successful
Education	5	4	1
Medical Subjects	5	4	1
Engineering / Technology	16	13	3
Agriculture, Veterinary Studies, Forestry	5	4	1
Science / Mathematics	192	155	37
Social Sciences	487	397	90
Languages	487	396	91
(of which Classics	139	119	20)
Arts other than Languages	465	378	87
of which History	314	244	70)

Sources: derived from *Civil Service Recruitment of Graduates 1974 and 1975*, London, Civil Service Commission.

the areas of political interfacing and administrative coordination from a literary élite more towards a scientific élite, by dint of the fact that those unsuccessful in the examination would find themselves in industry, etc. and, hopefully, since they will prove able people, at the top. In other words, as a result of this action we would expect the consequences to work their way through from the central administration into industry, commerce or academia through a sort of 'manpower multiplier' effect. One could thus release able graduate manpower into the economy in proportion to the sector preferences by the Civil Service in its recruitment of administrative grade trainees. However, to have any significant effect upon the choice of subject to be studied at university by school leavers a minimum of 51 per cent 'reserved graduate occupations' in that grade would have to be set aside for scientists and technologists.

The Civil Service corps today submits to the rigours of initiation in specialist procedures — administrative, political and judicial — generalists whose background may be steeped in the turpitudes of the later Roman Emperors or whose interests centre on the dubious sexual mores of Lord Castelreagh. But there is no reason on Earth why the same mysteries should not be revealed to those whose interests may lie in stress and load bearing factors, or which revolve around the waltzing orbits of the atom.

6. Concealed assumptions behind British binary policy in higher education

No one disputes that Britain now faces a twin and contradictory crisis. On the one hand, the need for better trained scientific manpower in industry. On the other, the drying up of the wherewithal, financially speaking, to provide it. Such a situation calls for a different and perhaps more effective solution than the ones we have hitherto embraced. Economic recession — like hanging — should concentrate the mind wonderfully.

So far, the assumptions that have governed British educational policy in relation to manpower planning have been surprisingly crude, given what both economic and sociological studies have taught us over the past century or more. If the education system has been expected to fulfill the tasks of both economic recovery and greater equality, equally, it has been expected that it should do so without the consequences touching over much upon our national administrative corps. Whereas, as we have noted earlier, the administrative body itself, through its prestige and its ability authoritatively to allocate the predominant values in society, in fact sets the outer bounds beyond which the consequences of such a policy, it would seem, ought not to tread. The solutions proposed to these problems have, as we have seen, been couched in a particularly restrictive mould. New institutions *per se* do not necessarily solve old problems.

If we look to emerging trends in the institutional aspects of education policy in Europe, one of the most interesting is the proposal for integrating higher education. The creation of the *Gesamthoch-schulen* (comprehensive universities) in Germany, the U68 reforms in the Swedish University, not to mention ideas currently being floated in Holland and Denmark — all tend in this direction. One may, if one so wishes, regard such developments as mere institutional reform which we have already argued is irrelevant to the British case. However, once one penetrates behind the structural aspects it is immediately apparent that what is involved is the maximization of the 'transformational capacity' of higher education. This may be accomplished in a number of ways. First, by providing a greater variety of courses in one institution so that students may make their choice of subject more in keeping with developing labour market and manpower demands. Second, and perhaps more significant in the long run, greater flexibility in the choice of length of course. The juxtaposition of both long and short cycle higher education in one complex institution will provide, it is thought, an even greater matching ability to both the individual's perceived educational needs and the ability to meet current market developments. Effectively, the transformational capacity of higher education establishments is enhanced through the possibility of students moving from long to short course study — a feature which the British binary system of higher education tends to restrict. Nevertheless, demands for an integrationist solution appear to be having some impact in Britain. The recent call for greater coordination between polytechnics and universities, albeit at regional level, is perhaps but a straw in the wind. It is only a part endorsement of the 'European' concept of integration. It falls far short of the staffing and administrative relationship between the French university faculty and the *Institut Universitaire de Technologie*. It falls far short of current Dutch proposals for the reform of their higher education system. These envisage a common system of financing and budgetary planning across the university and non-university sectors by means of a standardized allocation procedure according to specific disciplines, regardless of which side of the binary line they exist. If the problem does not lie after all with the traditional institutions of higher education, then — inertia apart — there can be no justification for maintaining the binary system.

In fine, having looked at some of the ways in which the current problems facing higher education are being tackled in Europe, it would seem that, if one is interested in the manpower planning aspects of education, it is probably true to say that neither sector, be it university or be it non-university — is flexible enough on its own to meet the pressing needs of the day, let alone of the future.

Summary

To sum up: this study of the influence of new European structures in higher education upon the equality of educational opportunity has produced conclusions reaching further than the original brief. Some, as we have shown, are particularly relevant to the debate in the UK on the continuance of the binary system of higher education. We have also cast some light on the failure of new structures, just as much as the old in the UK, to generate sufficient high grade engineers and applied scientists to sustain industrial and economic needs. The first conclusion is that problems which, on first sight, appear to be educational, turn out on examination to reflect values that are deeply entrenched among those controlling recruitment to the permanent Civil Service in the UK. The second conclusion which embodies the first is that more general proposition which states 'Old problems may need to be posed in new terms.' In this context, we postulated two new notions: the first, that of 'transformational capacity'; the second, the concept of the 'reserved graduate occupations' in the Civil Service as a powerful determinant in the context of both secondary and higher education, upon curriculum, staffing and student preferences. From this premise we argued that the shortage of higher ability graduate engineers in the UK lies even more squarely in the hands of government than has usually been supposed. In Europe, as in Britain, the government service's own concept of what makes the educated generalist, exerts a powerful influence on the whole nation's curricular patterns in education. Only in Britain does that concept and those patterns ignore so utterly and so consistently the values of science and technology.

S.J.
G.N.

REFERENCES

1. OCDE, *The Development of Secondary Education*, Paris, 1969.
2. James A. Perkins, and Barbara Baird, (eds) *Higher Education, From Autonomy to Systems*, New York, 1972, ICED.
3. Dorothea Furth, 'Short cycle higher education: some basic considerations', *Short Cycle Higher Education: a Search for Identity*, Paris, 1973, OCDE, pp. 15–6.
4. OCDE, *Vers un Enseignement de Masse*, vol. 1, Paris, 1974 pp. 17–8.
5. I. Hecquet et C. Verniers, *Evolution des flux d'étudiants dans l'enseignement supérieur*, Institut d'Education, in press.
6. G. Neave, *Paths to Glory: the development of secondary and higher education — Scotland, a case study*. Edinburgh, 1975, (typewritten) Centre for Educational Society, esp. Ch. 6.
7. G. Neave, *loc. cit.*
8. G. Neave, *op. cit.*
9. Hecquet et Verniers, *op. cit.*, p. 15.
10. *Loc. cit.*
11. *Loc. cit.*
12. Council of Europe Committee for Higher Education and Research. *Present Situation and Trends in Tertiary Education*: document CCC / ESR (75) 65, Strasbourg, 1975, (mimeo), p. 7.
13. On this see Richard Layard and Claus Moser, *The Politics of Robbins: A Level and After*, London, 1969, Penguin.
14. *Present situation and trends . . . op. cit.*, p. 12.
15. N.E. McIntosh and A. Woodley 'The Open University and secondary chance education', *Paedagogica Europaea*, vol. 2, 1974, p. 85.
16. Council of Europe Committee for Higher Education and Research, *Study on employment prospects for university graduates in the Netherlands*: document CCC / ESR (75) 50, Strasbourg, 1975, (mineo) p. 3.
17. *Ibid.*, p. 4.
18. Council of Europe Committee for Higher Education and Research, *Present Situation and Trends in Tertiary Education: the Netherlands*: document CCC / ESR (75) 57, Strasbourg, 1975, (mimeo), p. 3.
19. *Study on Employment Prospects . . . op. cit.*, p. 6.
20. Council of Europe Committee for Higher Education and Research, *Present Situation and Trends in Tertiary Education in Norway*: document CCC / ESR (75) 53, Strasbourg, 1975 (mimeo), pp. 2–3.
21. *Ibid.*, p. 3.
22. *Ibid.*, p. 2.
23. *Vide supra*, pp.
24. Council of Europe Committee for Higher Education and Research, *Present Situation and Trends in Tertiary Education in the United Kingdom*: document CCC / ESR (75) 54, Strasbourg, 1975, (mimeo) p. 1.
25. G. Neave, *Flows from secondary to post-secondary education in Scotland — 1962, 1970, 1972: report to the Scottish Education Department —* Edinburgh, 1975 (typewritten) Centre for Education Sociology.
26. *Employment Prospects for the Highly Qualified*, HMSO, 1974.

27. Quoted in *Present situation . . . in the United Kingdom, op. cit.*, p. 5.
28. *Council of Europe Newsletter*, 4 / 74.
29. *Council of Europe Newsletter*, 1 / 75.
30. On this see John Pratt and Tyrell Burgess. *Policy and Practice, the Colleges of Advanced Technology*, London, 1970, Allen Lane.
31. Hecquet et Verniers, *op. cit.*, pp. 20—2.
32. J.L. Quermonne, 'Place and role of University Institutes of Technology in the new French Universities'. In: D. Furth (ed) *Short Cycle Higher Education, op. cit.*, pp. 219, 225.
33. Hans Ulrich Simon in *Gesamthochschule: Studentische Politik*, Bad Godesberg, 1975, Forschungsinstitut der Friedrich-Ebert-Stiftung, pp. 73—81.
34. Conversation with Professor Gunther Hartfiel, Head of Department of Social Studies and Education, *Gesamthochschule Kassel*, 24th November 1975.
35. Ingjald Ø Sørheim, 'The Norwegian Regional Colleges'. In: Furth (ed), *op. cit.*, pp. 60—3.
36. Olav Magnusson, *Between School and Work*, Paris, 1976.
37. Jeremy Tunstall, *The Open University Opens*, London 1974, Routledge & Kegan Paul, p. ix.
38. N.E. McIntosh and A. Woodley, 'The Open University and second chance education: an analysis of the social and educational background of Open University Students', *Paedagogica Europaea*, vol. 2, 1974, p. 85.
39. *A Plan for Polytechnics and Other Colleges*, London, 1966. HMSO, p. 5.
40. *Loc. cit.*
41. *Ibid.*, p. 8.
42. John Pratt and Tyrell Burgess, *The Polytechnics: a report*, London, 1974, Pitmans, pp. 110—112.
43. D. Furth, *Short Course Higher Education, op. cit.*, p. 15.
44. *Ibid.*, p. 160.
45. *Ibid.*, p. 163.
46. *Loc. cit.*
47. Torsten Husén, *Talent, Equality and Meritocracy*, The Hague, 1974, Martinus Nijhoff, p. 24.
48. Christopher Jencks, *Inequality: a reassessment of the effect of family and schooling in America*, New York, 1972, Basic Books.
49. *Group Disparities in Educational Participation and Achievement*, Paris, 1970, OECD.
50. Council of Europe Committee for Higher Education and Research, *Present situation and Trends in Tertiary Education in Sweden*, document, CCC / ESR (75) 58, Strasbourg, 1975, p. 4.
51. Michael-Yves Bernard, *Les IUT's*, Paris, 1970, Dunod, p. 45.
52. J.L. Boursin, *Les Instituts Universitaires de Technologie*, Paris, 1970, Bourdas, p. 31.
53. Boursin, *op. cit.*, p. 31.
54. J.L. Quermonne, 'The place and role of University Institutes of Technology in the new French Universities'. In: D. Furth, *op. cit.*
55. Conseil de l'Europe, *La Diversification de l'enseignement tertiaire*, Strasbourg, 1974, Conseil de la coopération culturelle, pp. 15—6.
56. Quoted in Tunstall, *The Open University Opens, op. cit.*, p. 9.
57. Naomi McIntosh "Open admission — an open door or a revolving door", *Universities Quarterly*, Autumn 1975.
58. John Pratt and Tyrell Burgess, *The Polytechnics: a report*, London, 1974.
59. See, for instance, Eric Robinson, *The New Polytechnics: a people's university*, London, 1969, Penguin.

60. 'The development of Two Year Post Secondary Schools in Yugoslavia' in Furth, *op. cit.*, p. 189.
61. *Ibid.*, p. 187.
62. Donald Swift, *Address to the British Section of the Comparative Education Society in Europe*, September 9th, 1975.
63. OCDE, *Group Disparities in educational participation and achievement*, vol. iv., Paris, 1970.
64. *Vide supra* pp.
65. Michel-Yves Bernard, *op. cit.*, pp. 140—1.
66. Secretariat d'Etat aux Universités, *Les caractéristiques de la croissance des effectifs universitaires d'après l'origine sociale des étudiants de 1960—1 à 1973—4*, Paris, 1975, p.,3.
67. *Ibid.*, p. 9.
68. Quoted in *ibid.*, p. 2.
69. Janina Markiewicz Lagneau, Michèle Netter et Jacques Lorieux, *Les Etudiants des IUT's en France*, Paris, 1973 OCDE.
70. *Ibid.*, p. 33.
71. *Ibid.*, p. 37.
72. *Ibid.*, p. 23.
73. *Ibid.*, p. 22.
74. *Ibid.*, p. 106.
75. *Ibid.*, p. 96.
76. Olaf Magnusson, *Between School and Work*, Paris, 1976 Institut d'Education.
77. Magnusson, *loc. cit.*
78. *Ibid.*, p. 14.
79. J. Whitburn, M. Mealing, C. Cox and S. Robinson, *Report on the Polytechnic Survey*, London, 1975, Polytechnic of North London, Department of Sociology (mimeo), p. 75.
80. *Ibid.*, p. 84.
81. Pratt and Burgess, *The Polytechnics, op. cit.*, p. 86.
82. Naomi McIntosh and Judith A. Calder, *A Degree of Difference: a study of the first years intake to the Open University of Great Britain*, Milton Keynes, 1975 (xerox), p. 113.
83. *Loc. cit.*
84. Allan Woodley and Naomi McIntosh, *People who decide not to apply to the Open University*, Milton Keynes, 1974 (xerox), p. 17.
85. Institut d'Education. *Educational Leave Policies in the European Economic Community: a report to the Carnegie Foundation*, Paris, 1975, (xerox).
86. McIntosh and Woodley, *op. cit.*, p. 15.
87. Naomi McIntosh and Allan Woodley, 'The Open University and second chance education: an analysis of the social and educational background of Open University students', *Paedagogica Europaea*, vol. 2, 1974, p. 96.
88. *Loc. cit.*
89. On this see Guy R. Neave, *How They Fared, op. cit.*, Appendix G and F, pp. 220ff.
90. McIntosh and Woodley, in *Paedagogica Europaea, op. cit.*, p.98.
91. Philippe Cibois and Janina Markiewicz Lagneau, *Bilan de l'enseignement supérieur court*, Paris, 1974, OCDE, *Table 1.2*, p. 13.
92. *Ibid.*, p. 60.
93. *Ibid.*, p. 73.
94. *Ibid.*, p. 85.
95. *Ibid.*, p. 108.
96. *Loc. cit.*

97. *Op. cit.*, p. 106.
98. *Loc. cit.*
99. *Ibid.*, p. 110.
100. George Brosan 'A polytechnic philosophy'. In: Brosan and Carter (eds) *Patterns and Policies in Higher Education*, London, 1971, Penguin, pp. 66—8.
101. *Vide supra* pp.
102. For this problem in a British context see Neave, *op. cit.*
103. *Vide supra* Chapter Three.
104. Council of Europe Committee for Higher Education and Research, *Present Trends and situation in tertiary education: the Netherlands*, document CCC / ESR (75) 57, Strasbourg 1975, mimeo.